I DO . . . I DID . . . I'M DONE!

♦ "Bigamy is having one husband too many. Monogamy is the same."—Erica Jong, divorced three times

♦ "I married at twenty-one, your typical college-sweetheart situation, where it's more of an excuse to get out of the house than anything."—David Letterman, divorced

♦ "Being divorced is like being hit by a Mack If you live through it, you start looki carefully to the right and to the l

♦ "For a while we pondered wh or get a divorce. We decided th is over in two weeks, but a divo ing you always have."—Woody Allen

♦ "I always say a girl must get married for love—and just keep on getting married until she finds it." —Zsa Zsa Gabor, married seven times

♦ "After my marriage, she edited everything I wrote. And what is more, she not only edited my works, she edited me!"—Mark Twain

FROM "I DO" TO "I'LL SUE"

JILL BAUER was only seventeen when she conducted her first interview—with Barbara Walters for her hometown newspaper. She is now a freelance writer who has written for and edited several magazines and newspapers in Florida, New York, and London. She lives in Miami Beach, Florida.

FROM "I DO" TO "I'LL SUE"

An Irreverent Compendium for Survivors of Divorce

Jill Bauer

A PLUME BOOK

PLUME
Published by the Penguin Group
Penguin Books USA Inc., 375 Hudson Street,
New York, New York 10014, U.S.A.
Penguin Books Ltd, 27 Wrights Lane,
London W8 5TZ, England
Penguin Books Australia Ltd, Ringwood,
Victoria, Australia
Penguin Books Canada Ltd, 10 Alcorn Avenue,
Toronto, Ontario, Canada M4V 3B2
Penguin Books (N.Z.) Ltd, 182–190 Wairau Road,
Auckland 10, New Zealand

Penguin Books Ltd, Registered Offices:
Harmondsworth, Middlesex, England

First published by Plume, an imprint of New American
Library, a division of Penguin Books USA Inc.

First Printing, April, 1993
10 9 8 7 6 5 4 3 2 1

Copyright © Jill Bauer, 1993
All rights reserved

 REGISTERED TRADEMARK—MARCA REGISTRADA

LIBRARY OF CONGRESS CATALOGING-IN-PUBLICATION DATA:
Bauer, Jill.
   From "I do" to "I'll sue" : an irreverent compendium for survivors
of divorce / Jill Bauer.
     p. cm.
   ISBN 0-452-26859-1 (pbk.)
   1. Divorce—Humor.   2. Divorce—United States—Humor.   I. Title.
HQ814.B38   1993
306.89′0207—dc20   92-30634
                                                                                              CIP

Printed in the United States of America
Set in Times Roman
Designed by Leonard Telesca

Without limiting the rights under copyright reserved above, no part of this publication may be
reproduced, stored in or introduced into a retrieval system, or transmitted, in any form, or by any
means (electronic, mechanical, photocopying, recording, or otherwise), without the prior written
permission of both the copyright owner and the above publisher of this book.

For my parents,
Frank Bauer and Louise Bauer—my genesis and inspiration.

Contents

Acknowledgments

Special thanks to my sister, soul mate and best friend—
Joy Bauer.

My appreciation to my mother, Louise Bauer, for
teaching me the power of words. For listening with
intelligence, compassion, encouragement and wit.

I am also grateful to my grandmother—Hermine
Bauer—Laurie Bernstein, Peter Borland, Sandy
Choron—for bringing it all together with literary
saychel—Alexa Garbarino, Allan Kessler, Nancy and
Ed Newman, Benton Patterson, and Sam Srednick—for
passing along the music of life.

Introduction

A couple of years ago, I needed some answers. Why was divorce such a contentious, fast-growing, frenetic institution? And why were so many people doing such crazy, obsessive, sidesplitting, hair-raising things because of it?

My research began at a public library. I was looking for an amusing compilation of divorce anecdotes and facts. At the time, there were 600 books in print on the topic of divorce. They were all helpful in creating what we have here but none of them really expressed the chaos, fury, and yes—*humor* of divorce.

We all know that divorce isn't all fun and games. But if you're going through one of these calamities or if you know someone who is, you're aware that it's high time to laugh a little. Now, one might wonder what could possibly be funny about divorce. After two years of research, I assure you that men and women do some pretty hysterical things when it comes to splitting up.

From the New Jersey man who sawed his house in half to the Oakland woman who shot her husband for bowling a gutter ball— these real-life stories will open your eyes to the depraved, desperate and devious things they did for love. There is something about this battle of the sexes that brings out the beast in people.

But besides pointing out the lighter side of breaking up, you'll be comforted with thoughts from actors, authors, athletes, musicians, politicians, and world leaders in this collection of quotes, anecdotes, and facts.

At last, there *is* a book about divorce—the good, the sad, the factual, and the funny.

A Hers- and His-tory of Divorce

1174   Marie, Countess of Champagne, issues proclamation: "We declare that love cannot exist between two people who are married to each other. For lovers give to each other freely, under no compulsion; married people are in duty bound to give in to each other's desires."

"All the King's Women"

1527   Henry VIII, desiring a male heir, wishes to marry Anne Boleyn and annul his marriage to Katharine of Aragon. But Pope Clement VII, under the control of Katharine's nephew, Charles V, resists his demands for a divorce. Eventually (six years later), his marriage to Katharine is pronounced invalid.

1536   Indictment of Anne Boleyn cites coerced testimony that Anne had incest with her brother, George, and that she had been seen "alluring him with her tongue in the said George's mouth and the said George's tongue in hers." She was charged with treason, incest with her brother, and adultery (with four men). She was 28 years old when she was beheaded.

1536   Henry VIII marries Jane Seymour. In 1537, their son, Edward VI, is born. Jane dies 12 days later.

1540   Henry marries Anne of Cleves—the daughter of a powerful Protestant prince. He marries her for political reasons and, finding her dull and unattractive, divorces her that same year. He refers to her as "The Flanders Mare."

1540   Henry marries Catherine Howard. She is accused of adultery late in 1541 and subsequently beheaded.

1543   Catherine Parr becomes his sixth queen until his death in 1547.

(Another black mark on the marital record of Henry VIII as England celebrates the 500th year of his birth: Documents made public in 1991 show that he was virtually impotent after the third of his six marriages.)

1582   William Shakespeare marries Anne Hathaway, eight years his senior. Their marriage is known to be a troubled one among charges of cuckoldry, and it is rumored that William is trapped into marrying Anne.

1639   Puritans in Massachusetts grant the first divorce in America to Mrs. James Luxford, on grounds of bigamy. She is awarded Mr. Luxford's property and he is fined, placed in the stocks, then banished to England.

1675   Nell Gwynn, mistress of Charles II, accompanies him to Oxford, where her coach is attacked by an angry crowd in the mistaken belief that she is Louise de Kéroualle, another of Charles's mistresses and a Roman Catholic. Instantly realizing their mistake, she leans out of window and shouts, "Pray, good people, be civil; I am the *Protestant* whore."

1796   Napoleon and Josephine marry. Two days after the wedding Napoleon marches off to conquer Italy and she stays home and has affairs with other men. They stay together for 13 years but when Josephine is unable to get pregnant, their marriage is annulled. Napoleon marries an 18-year-old Austrian princess who bears him an heir. Josephine is left brokenhearted.

c.1847   John Ruskin's marriage to Euphemia ("Effie") Gray is unconsummated because "Ruskin is so appalled at the sight of her pubic hair that he is unable to bring himself to have relations with her."

1858   Charles Dickens and Catherine Hogarth separate after a 22-year marriage.

1874   Brigham Young is imprisoned until he pays Ann Eliza temporary alimony.

1877   The *Young* v. *Young* divorce case is dismissed by a judge who refuses to recognize Young's polygamous marriage to Eliza. Consequently, Ann Eliza Young fails to get a divorce decree and alimony, while Brigham Young fails in getting recognition of polygamous marriages. Young has a total of 27 wives.

1910   Katherine Mansfield marries a singing teacher 11 years her senior and abandons him the morning after her wedding night.

1910   Eighty-two-year-old Leo Tolstoy flees from his wife and dies in a railway station.

1910   The U.S. divorce rate is 8.8 per 100 marriages.

1911   Upton Sinclair sues his wife, Meta, for divorce after her extramarital affair with poet Harry Kemp. Meta is in search of "sexually vital men" as opposed to her "sexually inadequate husband." After several divorce hearings in New York, where statutes prevent Sinclair from getting a divorce, he travels to the Netherlands, where he obtains a migratory divorce.

1920   The U.S. divorce rate rises to 13.4 per 100 marriages.

1926   Hollywood legend Rudolph Valentino refuses to carry bride Jean Acker across the threshold; she locks him out of their honeymoon hideaway, sues for divorce.

1928   The U.S. divorce rate hits 16.5 per 100 marriages, twice the 1910 rate.

1931   Tommy Manville marries for first time.

1934   *The Gay Divorcee* is originally titled *The Gay Divorce,* until the Hays Office (the movie industry's official censor) rules that no divorce could be happy.

1935   On May 13 heiress Barbara Hutton divorces husband "Prince" Alexis Mdivani and declares, "I shall never marry again."

1935   On May 14 Barbara Hutton marries Count Haugwitz-Reventlow.

1937   Edward VIII, King of England, abdicates to marry 41-year-old, twice-divorced American Wallis Warfield Simpson; calls her "the woman I love."

1937   Matrimonial Causes Bill facilitates divorce in England.

1942   Supreme Court upholds Nevada divorces.

1943   Errol Flynn tried and acquitted of statutory rape; "in like Flynn" enters language as epitome of sexual success.

1947   Darryl Zanuck, the production chief of 20th Century-Fox, options the best-seller *Gentleman's Agreement* and sends a synopsis of the book to Joe Breen at the Hays Office. Breen's response: "We would like to state . . . that it is regrettable that the sympathetic lead in your story should be a divorced woman. . . . We have, of course, steadfastly refused to approve stories which contained an outright justification of divorce, and have endeavored to approve divorce in motion pictures only when it was obtained against the wishes and generally over the objection of the sympathetic lead."

1948   Ronald Reagan and Jane Wyman split, making Reagan the only divorced man elected to the presidency of the United States.

1954   Marilyn Monroe weds Joe DiMaggio.

1956   Marilyn Monroe weds Arthur Miller.

1958   Woody Allen and Harlene Rosen divorce.

1958   Charles Manson and Rosalie Jean Wallace divorce.

1959   Hugh Hefner and Millie Williams divorce.

1960   Tommy Manville marries for the twelfth and last time.

1960   Lucille Ball and Desi Arnaz divorce after a 20-year marriage.

1960   Norman Mailer stabs wife with kitchen knife, receives three-year suspended sentence after observation at Bellevue.

1964   Henry Kissinger and Ann Fleischer divorce.

1966   Jack Nicholson and Sandra Knight divorce.

1968   Richard Burton gives Elizabeth Taylor the 33-karat Krupp diamond.

1969   Frank Sinatra and Mia Farrow divorce.

1970   Woody Allen and Louise Lasser divorce.

1972   Elvis Presley and Priscilla Beaulieu Presley divorce.

1976   Elizabeth Ray, secretary to Congressman Wayne Hayes, reveals her sole duties consist of having sexual relations with her employer, says she's angry because he failed to invite her to his wedding.

1976   Elizabeth Taylor and Richard Burton divorce for the second time.

1977   Don Johnson and Melanie Griffith divorce.

1979   Michele Triolo sues Lee Marvin for "palimony."

1979 *Kramer vs. Kramer* is a box-office hit.

1979 Dustin Hoffman and Ann Byrne divorce.

1981 Ted Kennedy and Virginia Joan Bennett divorce.

1982 Roxanne and Herbert "Peter" Pulitzer divorce.

1983 Johnny Carson divorces for the third time.

1983 Paul Simon and Carrie Fisher divorce.

1984 Bjorn Borg and Mariana Simionescu divorce.

1984 Sting and Frances Tomelty divorce.

1986 Norman and Frances Lear divorce.

1986 *Heartburn* is a box-office hit.

1988 Bruce Springsteen and Julianne Phillips divorce.

1989 Steven Spielberg and Amy Irving divorce.

1989 Mike Tyson and Robin Givens divorce in the Dominican Republic.

1989 *The War of the Roses* is a box-office hit.

1990 Tom Cruise and Mimi Rogers divorce.

1991 Nick Nolte, 49, and wife Rebecca, 30, seek divorce in Los Angeles where they will share custody of their son, Brawley King Nolte.

1992 Nelson and Winnie Mandela
Jim and Tammy Faye Bakker
Ivan and Seema Boesky
Joan Lunden and Michael Krauss
William Masters and Virginia Johnson
Richard Dreyfuss and Jeramie Rain
Prince Andrew and Sarah Ferguson
Princess Anne and Captain Mark Phillips
file for divorce.

Early to Wed

"I wasn't prepared to be a good father or a good husband during
my first marriage. I didn't have the disposition, experience,
or maturity. I wasn't easy to live with."

—HARRISON FORD, divorced after a 17-year marriage

33 percent of women ⎱ who are divorced were
14 percent of men ⎰ married before the age of 20.

"I was fourteen years old and I didn't have the prom, the social
things. I went into one world and missed out on another. I
had so much so soon. That led to a lot of confusion because
I had a late start in life in terms of growing. Even though
I had experience and seen much, I was young and naive, so
guided that by the time I was thirty years old it was a whole
new world out there. I was so secluded and so sheltered
in a relationship that I didn't know how to interrelate with
people. . . . I lived in a cocoon."

—PRISCILLA PRESLEY, divorced from Elvis in 1973 after a six-year marriage;
she was 16 when Elvis brought her to live with him at Graceland.

No Kidding

Hal Warden, 12, married Wendy Chappell, 14, in Nashville but was divorced a month later as she claimed he "was acting like a 10-year-old." Hal, a construction worker at the time, was ordered to pay $30 a week to support their child; however, in a case that went all the way to the Tennessee Supreme Court of Appeals, the amount was reduced to $15 a week (the entire amount of Hal's allowance from his parents) when he quit to return to seventh grade. At 14, Hal married Catherine Trent, 15, but they divorced shortly after their daughter, Ashley, was born; Hal and Catherine had worked out a 50-50 split of Ashley's support.

In 1890 there were 12 divorced 14-year-old females and one divorced 14-year-old male.
In 1970 there were 1,900 divorced 14-year-old females and 1,800 divorced 14-year-old males.

"My first marriage didn't last very long. We were both too young. My wife was in her teens and so was I. I was 18 years old with all that responsibility. We didn't know what we were doing. It was mostly physical attraction. We had to be with each other. I imagined that I was going to be drafted and killed. I said, 'Oh, I'd better get on with life and have my life now' so that's what we did."

—GEORGE BENSON

"I married at 21, your typical college-sweetheart situation, where it's more of an excuse to get out of the house than anything."

—DAVID LETTERMAN, divorced

"It's part of growing up. I was 21 years old. I didn't know nothing about life, marriage and all that crap. . . ."

—MIKE TYSON, on divorce from Robin Givens

"I was married once, when I was 23 years old, to a girl
I met in school. I am not sorry to have been married. It
permitted me to have children and to have no curiosity about
it. But I do not think it will happen again."

—HUGH HEFNER, 1966. HEFNER, 65, married
28-year-old Kimberly Conrad in 1988.

"... It didn't work out. It was awful. Terrible! I'm older now,
and I hope that would never happen again. But I was only
in my early thirties and, I guess, kind of dumb."

—CHEVY CHASE, on his four-year marriage to Jacqueline Carlin

"We were young and impetuous. It was a very fervent time.
It was also real hairy.... We had a child. That was the last
thing either of us needed.... It was a college relationship.
I was going off to work in the theater but when my son
was born, we decided to give it a shot and marry. Look, I was
doing just a version of what my parents had done and what
all of our parents had done. We tried."

—TOM HANKS, divorced after a five-year marriage to actress
Samantha Lewes. He is now married to actress
Rita Wilson who he met on the set of *Volunteers*.

Divorces worldwide are highest for childless or single-
child couples who are between the ages of 25 and 29.
There is no rise in divorce among men in their forties
and fifties.

A seven-year study of 459 women in the Detroit area
concluded that women who married their first boyfriend were just as likely to have a successful marriage as
those who dated and waited.

"Hasty marriage seldom proveth well."

—SHAKESPEARE, *Henry IV*

"I got married at 20, and for me it was a drastic, positive change.... [I got married] to make other people comfortable."

> —SUSAN SARANDON, on marrying Chris Sarandon while attending Catholic University. They divorced in 1979 and she now lives with actor Tim Robbins.

"I feel like I woke up at 27. Things were going so quickly there, I feel like I should be 23.... I was a person who thought she knew everything she needed to know. Now I have great respect for anyone who's been here a day longer than I have."

> —ROBIN GIVENS, explaining that her 18-month marriage to boxer-rapist Mike Tyson equaled three years of regular living

"Men often marry in hasty recklessness and repent afterward all their lives."

> —MOLIÈRE, *Les Femmes Savantes*

Senior Splits

Old Milwaukee Brewing

Ida Stern, 91, and her husband Simon Stern, 97, of Milwaukee, Wisconsin, were divorced on February 2, 1984, in the circuit court of Milwaukee. They are the oldest recorded divorcées in history.

Cruisin' for a Bruisin'

Police in Miami charged a 90-year-old man with killing his 76-year-old bride of less than a week during an argument over whether the newlyweds should take a honeymoon cruise.

Old Testaments

An 84-year-old woman shot her 81-year-old husband in the leg with a .38-caliber revolver during an argument over her having kissed a pastor after church. "I tried to tell him it was in the Bible, but he kept pushing me and yelling," she told police, who charged her with assault with a deadly weapon.

The Big Bang

In Crete, Illinois, an 80-year-old man confessed to beating his wife of 57 years to death with a hammer. He told police that he suffered from a heart ailment and cataracts, was afraid he would die and wanted to avoid leaving his wife a widow.

"The more you beat your wife, the better will be the soup.
   Beat a woman with a hammer and you'll make gold.
   Beat your wife with the butt of an ax; if she falls down, sniffs and gasps, she is deceiving: give her some more.
   A wife is not a pot, she will not break so easily.
   A wife may love a husband who never beats her, but she does not respect him."

—RUSSIAN PROVERB

"I suppose 80 is the proper time for getting married because then you can be sure it will last."

—LAUREN BACALL

2.7 percent of women ⎫
3.3 percent of men   ⎬ age 75 and over are divorced.

Organ Grinder

In New Bedford, Massachusetts, a 77-year-old woman confined to a wheelchair was charged with murdering her 80-year-old husband.

Before he died, he told police his wife constantly hit him with a walking cane, a glass vase, and other objects over a three-day period. He added she didn't allow him to sleep during that time; when he tried, she grabbed his genitals and pulled, squeezed, and twisted them until he could no longer stand the pain. Investigators said his left foot was almost double its normal size and his genital area was "swollen to the size of a small balloon."

Twice the Rice

Celebrities Who Married the Same Person Twice

Desi Arnaz and Lucille Ball
Milton Berle and Joyce Matthews
Richard Burton and Elizabeth Taylor
David Carradine and Gail Carradine
Jon Hall and Racquel Torres
Freddie Karger and Jane Wyman
Don Johnson and Melanie Griffith
Stan Laurel [eight marriages to four wives]
Carroll O'Connor and Nancy Fields
George Peppard and Elizabeth Ashley
Bobby Riggs and Priscilla Wheelan
William Saroyan and Carol Marcus
George C. Scott and Colleen Dewhurst
Neil Simon and Diane Lander
Dick Smothers and Linda Smothers
Robert Wagner and Natalie Wood

"I don't have many regrets, except that I wasn't with Donny all my life. But maybe it's better the second time around. I've always loved him. He was my first love and we were always friends. There was this connection. And everything seems better because of all that."

—MELANIE GRIFFITH, on marrying Don Johnson twice

"The foundation exists for Melanie and me to grow old together."

—DON JOHNSON, on remarrying Melanie Griffith

50 percent of married women} would marry the same
77 percent of married men} person if they had to do it all over again.

IBM Compatible

After his divorce, Walter Davis listed with a London marriage service to find a new partner. The agency's computer searched through the thousands of names on file and came up with Ethel, his former wife, who had subscribed to the service. Obviously meant for each other, the two remarried in 1975.

"In 1942 I met her at last, in 1943 I married her; in 1949 I divorced her. In 1951 I married her again, I divorced her again in 1952, and then I didn't marry her anymore."

—WILLIAM SAROYAN, on ex-wife Carol Marcus who married Walter Matthau in 1959

Sister Sledge

Jurors convicted a 46-year-old woman of conspiracy to commit first-degree murder but acquitted her twin sister of charges that they helped kill the 85-year-old man each had married twice. Darlene Phillips of South Dakota was convicted. Delores Christenson was acquitted. Phillips received mandatory life in prison for the murder.

"Don't ask me about it. He got the divorce."
>   —ELIZABETH TAYLOR, 1976, on Richard Burton. Taylor and Burton
>   first married each other in 1964 and divorced in 1975.
>   Their second marriage ended in 1976.

34 percent of today's weddings involve a bride or groom who has been married before.

"Oh, don't worry about Alan. . . . Alan will always land on somebody's feet."
>   —DOROTHY PARKER; Parker and screenwriter Alan Campbell were
>   divorced for three years after their first 14-year marriage.
>   Their second marriage lasted until Campbell's death in 1963.

"I recommend marriage highly for everyone except me."
>   —JANE WYMAN; she had already been married and divorced once
>   before marrying and divorcing costar Ronald Reagan. Wyman
>   then married composer Fred Karger in 1952 and they divorced in
>   1954. They remarried in 1961 and divorced again in 1963.

"Many a man owes his success to his first wife, and his second wife to his success."

>   —JIM BACKUS

"One good husband is worth two good wives; for the scarcer things are, the more they're valued."

—BENJAMIN FRANKLIN

"And to make absolutely sure you get all the results possible from your ex, we will include, free, a bonus instruction booklet that tells you, among other things, how to use your ex-husband to control the behavior of your new husband. . . . Unlike any other close relationship in your life, you will never have to feel that your ex-husband is a real person with real feelings. This is known as the divorce effect. He is simply the sum of his less attractive parts: a sort of cartoon character—The Ex. . . . So call our toll-free number right now and take advantage of this great opportunity to get an ex of your own. Don't settle for having to listen to your best friend discuss hers. We offer one easy payment plan: Buy now, and pay for the rest of your life."

—DELIA EPHRON, *Funny Sauce*

"Christ saw a wedding once, the Scripture says, / And saw but one, 'twas thought, in all his days; / Whence some infer, whose conscience is too nice, / No pious Christian ought to marry twice."

—ALEXANDER POPE, *The Wife of Bath*

"There are four minds in the bed of a divorced man who marries a divorced woman."

—HAGGADAH, *Palestinian Talmud*

"Marriage is a lot like the army: everyone complains, but you'd be surprised at the large number that reenlist."

—JAMES GARNER, divorced from Lois Clark in 1980

40 percent of second marriages fail in the first four years.

"Remarriage is an excellent test of just how amicable your divorce was."

—MARGO KAUFMAN

"People who haven't spoken to each other for years are on speaking terms again today—including the bride and groom."

—DOROTHY PARKER, upon marrying Alan Campbell for the second time.

60-Year Sabbaticals

Sixty years after their first marriage, which lasted four years, Levi and Vinnie Greer remarried in 1978. During their long separation, both had had other partners, but one was divorced and the other was widowed. As a result, they found themselves free to marry each other again. Levi advised: "Never give up, never."

Nina Reynolds was 14 and Paul Tarvin 16 when the two high-school sweethearts eloped. When they returned home on their wedding day in 1927, their parents annulled the marriage and the two went their separate ways. Sixty-five years later, Nina and Paul got together by chance at her St. Cloud, Florida, home and decided to retie the knot. Said Tarvin: "I thought of her often over the years. After all, she was my first love."

"We are all amateurs at marriage the first time around; some of us are just luckier amateurs than others."

—JOHN LEONARD, columnist

"You know, the first time, you marry your mother, but the second time you marry yourself."

—AVERY CORMAN, from *Kramer vs. Kramer,* 1979

"I'm now married to my second wife. I had three, but her husband come and got the last one."

—SLEEPY JOHN ESTES, blues artist

"We knew we were committed. I'd been through a marriage once before. Leaving doesn't necessarily promote growth. It may. But the truth is, you'll end up dealing with wherever you left off in a relationship, the next time you have one."

—TED DANSON

"I knew Mayo [Bogart's first wife] was an alcoholic, and that Bogie was a very unhappy man. My only aim was to give Bogie a life he had never known before. And I succeeded."

—LAUREN BACALL, Humphrey Bogart's second wife

30 percent of women } say alcohol abuse by their
6 percent of men   } spouses is a cause of divorce.

"If you're married to a Crosby, you've got to drink."

—DIXIE LEE, on ex-husband Bing Crosby

"My first wife never complimented me on the way I look, but Carol says I am the handsomest man in the world. Believe it or not, that made a big change in my life."

—WALTER MATTHAU; he divorced Grace Johnson after a 10-year marriage and has been married to Carol Saroyan since 1959

"In the course of his sermon [the preacher], asserted that the Savior was the only perfect man who had ever appeared in this world, also that there was no record in the Bible, or elsewhere, on any perfect woman having lived on this earth. Whereupon there arose in the rear of the Church a persecuted-looking personage who said, 'I know a perfect woman, and for the last six years.' 'Who was she?' asked the minister. 'My husband's first wife,' replied the afflicted female."

—ABRAHAM LINCOLN

> 63 percent of women ⎫ in second marriages would
> 82 percent of men ⎬ marry the same person if they
>   ⎭ had it to do again.

"She was living in the house anyway."
> —BILLY ROSE; Rose divorced swimming star Eleanor Holm in 1956
> to marry Joyce Matthews, and the newspapers announced
> it as the "New War of the Roses." They were divorced 37
> months after the wedding and remarried two years later.

"We went straight from the altar onto the rocks."
> —MILTON BERLE; he was married to Joyce Matthews for six years
> until their divorce in 1947. They married each other again
> in 1949 and divorced 10 months later.

Love on the Rocks

A Pittsburgh man on why he was apparently throwing rocks at his
wife, who was struggling not to drown in the Kanawha River: "I
was trying to drive her back to shore."

"Here's to matrimony, the high sea for which no compass has
yet been invented!"

> —HEINE

"Alcestis had exercised a mysterious attraction and then
an unmysterious repulsion on two former husbands, the second
of whom had to resort to fatal coronary disease to get away
from her."

> —KINGSLEY AMIS

"I got married the second time in the way that, when a murder is committed, crackpots turn up at the police station to confess the crime."

—DELMORE SCHWARTZ

Double Trouble

In Syracuse, New York, a 34-year-old man who beat his first wife to death in 1977 admitted in 1984 to stabbing his second wife of less than a year in the chest while she was sleeping. When she awoke and started fighting back, he hit her on the head with a board, then had sex with her before calling an ambulance an hour later. According to police, when they arrived he said, "I stabbed my wife. I am on parole for killing my first wife, and I know I am going to get in trouble for this."

"Second marriages, unless the first one has been dissolved by death, are crimes."

—POPE LEO XII, 1880

"The graveyards are full of women whose houses were so spotless you could eat off the floor. Remember the second wife always has a maid."

—HELOISE CRUSE

"The wife in curlpapers is replaced by the wife who puts on lipstick before she wakens her husband."

—MARGARET MEAD

"When a woman marries again, it is because she detested her first husband. When a man marries again, it is because he adored his first wife. Women try their luck; men risk theirs."

—OSCAR WILDE, *The Picture of Dorian Gray*

A woman has a 78 percent chance of remarrying; a man 83 percent; 7 percent of women remarry within one year, 35.7 percent within three, 49.4 percent within five years.

"Women who have been happy in a first marriage, are the most apt to venture upon a second."

—JOSEPH ADDISON, *The Drummer*

Player Queen: "The instances that second marriage move / Are base respects of thrift / but not of love."

—SHAKESPEARE, *Hamlet*

"He who has not married a second time is never really poor."

—CHINESE PROVERB

Writing Wrongs

One man bought his wife the Sunday paper for her twenty-first birthday. Another, a doctor, caressed his wife's face and told her, "I know just where to press to break every bone in your face." These tales of horror are among the entries Simon & Schuster received for its First Wives Club Consumer Contest. The company, publisher of *The First Wives Club* by Olivia Goldsmith, a novel about three women dumped by their husbands for slim, young "trophy wives," asked women to write an essay on just how their ex-husbands done 'em wrong. Among the tales:

- Carolyn of Redwood City, California, was sitting on the couch after an exhausting trip to Disneyland with the kids when her architect husband informed her they had "irreconcilable architectural differences."

- Darlene of Tucker, Georgia, wrote that her husband would slap her on the chest at night and say, "If I'm not asleep, you're not asleep." When she put on some extra pounds, he would warn, "You could get diabetes and they'll cut your legs off."

First prize was a $1,500 gift certificate from Cartier.

"Doctors and lawyers must go to school for years and years, often with little sleep, and at great sacrifice to their first wives."
—ROY BLOUNT, JR.

Occupational Hazards

"Cary Grant was the most important thing in my life—more important than *anything*. That was the big flaw. I pushed aside everything that I'd desired to make him happy."

—DYAN CANNON

"Bogie insisted that I be a wife first—and an actress second. He believed that marriage was a responsibility that you worked at. He wasn't a male chauvinist pig, but he believed a wife was a wife *first*—and a jobholder second."

—LAUREN BACALL

"I would have carried on with my career, but I put my energy into him. . . . I was sick, confused, frustrated, disgusted, disbelieving."

—RAYNOMA SINGLETON, on ex-husband Berry Gordy

"Marriage is not for me because I have no time for the husband's role. I have no time to give up variety, adventure, my work. I am married to my work, to my philosophy, and this is a marriage that does not permit any divorce."

—HUGH HEFNER, 1966

"I hadn't spent a lot of time at home. I just used it as a pit stop."

> —SAM DONALDSON, on his marriage to Billy Kay Donaldson. Donaldson, 55, was married for the third time in 1989 to 33-year-old journalist Jan Smith.

"I'm sure people will say, 'If these two people can't get along, who can?' [They have] differences in the goals each has for the balance of their lives. They had little time for personal interests, family or friends. But they will continue to work together and be great friends."

> —WILLIAM YOUNG, son-in-law of sex researchers William Masters and Virginia Johnson. Masters and Johnson filed for divorce in February 1992 after a 21-year marriage.

"My love for her remains undiminished . . . [but] we have mutually agreed that a separation would be best for each of us."

> —NELSON MANDELA, announcing in April 1992 that he and his wife of 33 years, Winnie Mandela, had agreed to separate.

"It's tough to find a secure black man who doesn't feel threatened that your career might serve to deball him."

> —DIAHANN CARROLL, twice divorced and now separated from Vic Damone after a four-year marriage.

"Gus and I had a very strong physical attraction for one another, but it wasn't enough to sustain the marriage. One of the major problems was, of course, my success. I was working, but he wasn't. Gus couldn't cope with it . . . my money, the house, all the pretty things that he couldn't afford and that I bought.

"Men can't seem to take this. I have had to kind of play down achievements because in both marriages I didn't want to be better than my man. I'm not saying it's impossible to find a man who can take this kind of thing. My trouble

is I've always been with a man who's struggling to get
on in his career."

—Goldie Hawn

"Goldie did everything she could to hold the marriage
together, but no matter how hard she tried to reassure me
I just couldn't see why she needed me."

—Gus Trikonis, Goldie Hawn's ex-husband

57 percent of husbands whose wives are unsuccessful at
work are satisfied with their marriages.
52 percent of wives whose husbands are unsuccessful at
work are satisfied with their marriages.

"I don't think fifty-fifty relationships exist. Men have an incredible
variety of options. It's much harder for a woman to do both
things. I think traditional relationships work best. I grew
up with the idea that I was supposed to have the bastard
children of great artists and powerful men or something, and
count myself among the courtesans. Then the rules changed
in midstream, but I still think great artists are the most
interesting. Like my ex-husband. But you have to constantly
arrange yourself around them, and that can take up a lot of
energy. I mean, you don't go, 'Why don't you cook dinner
tonight, dear, for a change, instead of writing a great song?'
I loved what he did with words. But I wanted some of that,
too."

—Carrie Fisher, on ex-husband Paul Simon

"Fame cost me my family. Now I'm sleeping with a stranger
called success."

—Robert Blake; in 1977, at the height of his acting career,
wife Sondra Kerr left him

"My success is the cause of my divorce. It caused me

embarrassment and problems I never anticipated. Ross really wanted the kind of celebrity that I now have, and I wanted to do really good occasional parts in musicals. The irony is that I got what he wanted, and he got what I was after. I think that if things had worked out the way that we wanted them to, we would still be together."

—LONI ANDERSON, 1981, on ex-husband Ross Brickell

"It wasn't my idea to end the relationship with Sally [Field]. She decided she'd like to go off and be a movie star. I wanted to have a house like *Leave It to Beaver.*"

—BURT REYNOLDS, 1981

79 percent of wives whose husbands are successful at work are satisfied with their marriages.
76 percent of husbands whose wives are successful at work are satisfied with their marriages.

"People have attached my name to my wives' success rather than to those movies I made that were good. When someone once called me Mr. Bardot, I knew there might be a bad side to all this."

—ROGER VADIM, divorced from Brigitte Bardot, Jane Fonda, and Catherine Deneuve

"I had very little self-esteem. I was depressed often. I tried very hard to be involved in things that brought me pleasure. But it wasn't enough. . . . Emotionally, I was a nonperson. I could not *feel* my identity. . . . Unless she is nailed to her husband, an industry wife is looked *through,* never looked *at.*"

—FRANCES LEAR, divorced three times, most recently from TV/ film producer Norman Lear

"I started my career as the daughter of [director] Jules Irving.

I don't want to finish it as the wife of Steven Spielberg
or the mother of Max."

—AMY IRVING

"I was immature and selfish and focused on becoming an actress.
I got married in part because I thought that's what I should
do. It lasted about two years. . . ."

—KELLY MCGILLIS

"To me actresses are the most unattractive women on the face
of the earth. They're so neurotic and needy. You can't just
trust them and they're big babies."

—MICKEY ROURKE; Rourke, 39, divorced actress Debra Feuer and
married 23-year-old actress-model Carré Otis in 1992

"Serious actresses shouldn't have any children unless
they're willing to give up their careers. The belief that a
woman can have everything—career, husband, children—is a
delusion. . . . It can't be done. Look at me. Obviously I marry
weak men or men are weaker than I am. In time they come
to resent me, my position, my earnings, my publicity, my
power. They accuse me of being arrogant, domineering, a castrator.
To keep me in line, they rough me up or they cheat on me
with other dames, or both. The answer for actresses like
me is to take lovers, not husbands."

—BETTE DAVIS, 1989

"I couldn't love him as I once did so I finally gave him my
permission to divorce me. His grounds were that I neglected
him for my career and that I read in bed, and in the final
analysis I guess he was right."

—BETTE DAVIS, on her first divorce

"Of course he was selfish . . . but he was absolutely devoted
to learning his trade."

—LILLI PALMER, Rex Harrison's third of five wives

"That son of a bitch is acting even when he takes his pajamas off."

> —CAROLE LOMBARD, on her marriage to William Powell

"My responsibilities to my family come first. If I have to make a choice, acting loses out."

> —AUDREY HEPBURN, divorced twice

"I know you think show biz is all I care about, but you see that's where you're wrong, doll. You're all I care about. . . . If I ever lost you my dreams would end."

> —ANDREW DICE CLAY, in love letters made public by ex-wife Kathy Swanson, who sued him for $6 million

"Music is my mistress and she plays second fiddle to no one."

> —DUKE ELLINGTON, divorced twice

"If you commit your brains and heart to another, you can no longer fight, and I need to fight."

> —JULIO IGLESIAS, divorced in 1978, never remarried

"The easiest kind of relationship for me is with ten thousand people. The hardest is with one."

> —JOAN BAEZ, divorced from activist David Harris

"When we were first married I was always asked, 'How do two superpersonalities get along?' And I'd say, 'We're very quiet.' When I'd want to say, 'We don't get on. We're just trying not to kill one another.' "

> —COLLEEN DEWHURST, on George C. Scott. After two marriages, one divorce and innumerable separations, they were divorced again in 1972.

A U.S. Census survey for the years 1887–1906 determined the occupations of about 75 percent of the husbands involved in divorce cases. The data indicated:
Actors and professional showmen exhibited the highest rate of divorce.
Musicians and teachers of music ranked second.
Commercial travelers were in third place.
Farmers and clergymen were at the bottom of the list.

"I've got a rock-and-roll life-style and Perri's got a burgeoning acting career. When I was home, she was working. When she was home, I was at the studio. . . . It is an amicable split, and we are sharing the responsibilities of raising our son."

—BILLY IDOL

"Rock-and-roll wives. . . . I hate 'em. Fortunately, there's only a couple of 'em around, but honestly, I don't know how they have the nerve to continue in the face of their appalling failure."

—MICK JAGGER, divorced from Bianca Jagger

"I realized I couldn't give him the kind of adulation he got from his fans, and he *needed* that adulation desperately. Without it he was nothing."

—PRISCILLA PRESLEY, on ex-husband Elvis

"In order to talk to him, I had to send telegrams."

—ALICE FAYE, on divorcing singer Tony Martin in 1939

Call Girl

Kawasaki, Japan, police arrested Toyoko Terahashi, 26, in 1988 for having made as many as 100,000 crank telephone calls to her ex-husband at his office over a two-year period. As many as 200 calls per day may have been made. When police arrived at her home to arrest her, she was talking to her husband. Police overheard her yell into the phone (in Japanese), "You idiot!" She said her monthly phone bill sometimes approached half her monthly salary.

"We'll divorce around each other's schedules. It seems only right. We got married around each other's schedules."
—PENNY MARSHALL, after a nine-year marriage to Rob Reiner

"It was a tough divorce because the business and the marriage got mixed together."
—SONNY BONO, on Cher

"Nowadays marriage like everything else is strictly business, and business is pressure."
—PETER USTINOV, *Romanoff and Juliet*

"Once a girl marries [a businessman], he wraps himself up in business again."
—BARBARA HUTTON

52 percent of executive women ⎱ are single or
4 percent of executive men ⎰ divorced

"Your ambition and her boredom—these were two of the main spears in the side of your marriage. Twist one and the other turned with it. Because you earned a lot of money, she didn't have to work. Because she didn't have to work, she nearly choked on her freedom. Your money made possible her boredom. . . . She began to resent the time you spent at your desk; you, knowing her resentment, began to resent the time you spent away from it. Twist one spear and the other turned with it."

—JOSEPH EPSTEIN, *Divorced in America*

"Never worry about women. Just try and be kind and good and think in their head and make them happy. If they are bitches you can always dump them. Most women aren't bitches except when they are made so by men. Man should do his work and love that the most; then his woman and his children, then his friends."

—ERNEST HEMINGWAY, married four times

16 percent of wives
34 percent of husbands } are focused primarily on their work rather than on their relationships with their spouses.

"He loved only one thing—his painting. Not his woman, not his children."

—FRANÇOISE GILOT, on Pablo Picasso

"We honor each other and each other's work and each other's magic."

—HELEN FRANKENTHALER, artist, divorced from artist Robert Motherwell

"I am incredibly sad about him, not because our marriage is over, but sad as a writer because all the attention he has garnered in the past two years has been about Salman Rushdie. . . . The great fallacy he committed was to think he was the issue."

—MARIANNE WIGGINS; Wiggins was a notable writer when she married Salman Rushdie in January 1988. But when Rushdie's book *The Satanic Verses* was published a year

later, her career was overshadowed. She joined her husband
in hiding when he received death threats because of
the book, but announced in July 1989—about the time
her fourth novel, *John Dollar,* was published—that they
had separated. When they filed for a divorce Wiggins cited
"ideological differences."

"After my marriage she edited everything I wrote. And what
is more—she not only edited my works—she edited me!"

—MARK TWAIN

"When Ava got divorced she called me and told me I could
marry her, but it was too late. The truth is I couldn't have
gone on with her. She didn't leave me any time for my bulls."

—LUIS MIGUEL DOMINGUIN, Spanish bullfighter, recalling the end of
his 1954 affair with Ava Gardner

"It proves that no man can be a success in two national
pastimes."

—OSCAR LEVANT, on the Joe DiMaggio/Marilyn Monroe divorce

"The futility and frustrations of the Mets were enough to
destroy any marriage."

—DANI TORRE, on why she divorced former New York Mets
manager Joe Torre

"You'd think I was the only guy in America to ever get
a divorce."

—PETE ROSE; Rose's divorce and paternity suit in 1979
created so much negative publicity that
the Cincinnati Reds did not renew his contract

"For most ballplayers, all getting married means is that now
they have to hide their datebooks."

—DON KOWET, *Sport,* 1974

"I myself am convinced that my career as a tennis player

will come to an end the moment I feel as much for a girl as I do for that little white ball."

> —BJORN BORG, before meeting Mariana Simionescu, whom he later divorced

"[He] was so into tennis he forgot I was there. [He] was hell to live with."

> —MARIANA SIMIONESCU, on ex-husband Bjorn Borg

Feelings . . . Oh, Oh, Oh, Feelings

"Even though there was pain as a result of those years, we had a wonderful daughter together. Cary was very special. I loved him with all my heart, with all my soul, with all my mind, and I will always be grateful that we married. I learned a lot from him. They weren't wasted years."
> —DYAN CANNON, after a three-year marriage to Cary Grant

"He was the love of my life. It is like a death to deal with. It's very, very difficult."
> —MADONNA, on divorcing Sean Penn after a four-year marriage

"I don't know if you've ever been divorced, but divorces are awful regardless of the circumstances. What I came to know is that people who are suffering or are in bad shape are very selfish, they don't have anything to give."
> —MIMI ROGERS, divorced from Tom Cruise

"I would have died if we hadn't gotten married, I wanted him so badly, I loved him so much, and nothing in the world could have prevented our coming together—just as nothing in the world could have prevented our parting as we did."
> —GLORIA VANDERBILT, on Leopold Stokowski, her second husband

"I don't like people; I don't love my neighbor. Every time
I put any faith in love or friendship, I come through with deep
wounds. Today I am truly a person not open to relationships.
I am deeply lonely, alone. I enjoy life, up to a point, but
I no longer have dreams. Death and old age are events which
I accept and await with all feasible serenity. To a certain extent
at times I make of them the purpose of living."

—MARLON BRANDO, divorced three times

"Divorce should be declared a form of insanity, or a communicable
disease. I have seen no one walk out of a divorce unmarked;
it makes you a different person. You can enter the sinister
cocoon as a butterfly and stagger out later as a caterpillar
doomed to walk under the eye of a spider. Or you can reverse
the process. There are no laws of nature that apply—only laws
of suffering, different for each individual."

—PAT CONROY, 1978

"It was real hard to be around friends who were couples. I
would feel jealous of people who cared about each other. . . .
Is this the single life? It stinks. I can function. Just don't
leave me alone at twilight—that's the loneliest time."

—PENNY MARSHALL, 1980

"He had treated her badly, he decided, but he had not caused
her to love him. Love. What a contemptible word. It should
be abolished, especially since it did not accurately describe
an enduring emotion. He had loved Barbara. Once he had told
her, long ago, that love was just God's way of randomly splitting
two people and letting them find themselves. When they
did, they were one. That was love. That was, he thought,
now, unmitigated bullshit. No, he corrected himself, that gave
it too much dignity. Love was a fart."

—THE WAR OF THE ROSES, novel by Warren Adler, 1981

> 56 percent of women ⎱ say emotional abuse is a cause
> 25 percent of men ⎰ of divorce.

"My possessiveness and fear of losing her brought about the
very condition I feared: the loss of her."
                              —CARY GRANT, on Virginia Cherrill

"Gary Merrill broke my heart. If I ever hear those wedding
bells again, I will scream with laughter and I will wear black."
                              —BETTE DAVIS

"The day he went away he left the seat up. . . . And I was
too lonely to put it down."
                              —OGDEN NASH, censored line from one of his plays

"How do you know when love is gone? If you said that you
would be there at seven and you get there by nine, and
he or she has not called the police yet—it's gone."
                              —MARLENE DIETRICH

"I have never loved anyone for love's sake, except, perhaps,
Josephine—a little."
                              —NAPOLEON, on ex-wife

"The break with human love remains somewhere inside, and
at times, under rain clouds, it aches like an amputation."
                              —ELIZABETH HARDWICK, *Seduction and Betrayal*

"I always tell my friends when they're feeling too secure,
go get married. Go get involved in something you can't possibly
control."
                              —NICK NOLTE, divorced three times

"A Roman divorced from his wife, being highly blamed
by his friends, who demanded, 'Was she not chaste? Was she

not fair? Was she not fruitful?' holding out his shoe, asked
them whether it was not new and well made. 'Yet,' added
he, 'none of you can tell where it pinches me.' "

—PLUTARCH, *Life of Aemilius Paulus*

> **60 percent of women** ⎱ say that unhappiness is a cause
> **47 percent of men** ⎰ of divorce

"Divorce is the psychological equivalent of a triple coronary
bypass. After such a monumental assault on the heart, it takes
years to amend all the habits and attitudes that led up to
it."

—MARY KAY BLAKELY

"To have felt too much is to end in feeling nothing."
—DOROTHY THOMPSON, on waiting in the Woodstock, Vermont,
courthouse for a divorce from Sinclair Lewis in 1942

"I'm supposed to be a hermit, a loner nursing a broken heart
because I lost Robert Taylor. . . . My divorce from Taylor was
sixteen years ago. If I'd been holding a torch that long by
now my arm would have withered."

—BARBARA STANWYCK, 1990

"Valerie and I have had a tumultuous relationship, back and
forth for a very long time. We went through amazing times.
Horrible times. . . . But right now I'm moving through my
personal life like a hemophiliac in a razor factory."
—ROBIN WILLIAMS, on his divorce from Valerie Velardi in 1988

"I believe the marriage is stone dead. I don't think there
is animosity between them. It's worse than that. They just
don't care anymore. It's just indifference."
—A BUCKINGHAM PALACE SOURCE on Prince Charles
and Princess Diana

"Joe and I were cut from the same cloth. He stuffed his
feelings the way I did. We never had arguments, just silences.
I would keep grievance lists in my head, and I'm sure he did
the same thing. We were on parallel lines. That just kills
a relationship.

"When Joe and I parted ways in 1982, most of the pain
had already taken place—like a slow ripping away of a very
sticky Band-Aid on a hairy spot."

> —CAROL BURNETT, on divorce from producer Joe Hamilton
> after a 19-year marriage

"There were a lot of sweet, sweet moments in our shared life.
But now it was obvious to both of us that it was over. Why
do people get divorced? Why do people get married? What
went wrong? I was desperate for answers...."

> —KIRK DOUGLAS, on divorce from Diana Darrid

"Our marriage hasn't been a bed of roses! Hell, we went
through some pretty rough stretches not so long ago....
During one rough stretch, I didn't think I was up to it anymore.
Sometimes you get terminally irritated, and at one point I just
packed up and left."

> —PAUL NEWMAN, divorced from Jacqueline Witte and
> married to Joanne Woodward since 1958

"I was in love both times. To be in love with anything is the
only reason to become that obsessive. I try to get consumed
by anything that I feel is so unique, so wonderful. And
when you're consumed, and you're in the eye of the hurricane,
you can't see everything swirling around on the outside. So
love is almost like a hurricane. It can be very wonderful
and very destructive."

> —SYLVESTER STALLONE, divorced twice

"When you can't remember why you hurt, that's when you're
healed. When you have to work real hard to re-create the
pain, and you can't quite get there, that's when you're
better."

> —JANE FONDA

"My mother was sad, although she could be gay, very lively, very much fun. Because she was so in love with my father, and because he was very powerful, I think it was impossible for her to get over that [love], even after they separated and she'd gone to live in London. Because of him, it was hard for her to fall in love with anybody else. I know what it's like to have someone with that much power and charisma in your life because, when it's over, it's never really over."

—ANJELICA HUSTON, after her 17-year relationship
with Jack Nicholson

"We doubled our loneliness by marrying."

—JEAN COCTEAU

"I have always been sitting on a great store of anger. All my wives have told me that."

—NEIL SIMON, divorced twice

"First it's like anything bad you can say comes out. I never slammed him publicly. But I went through a hostile period. My heart was really broken. You can be a bitch until your heart's broken, and when your heart's broken, you're a superbitch about everything except that. . . . And then I went through a period where I never would have known I was even married to the guy. It was like that part of my life did not exist. Four years. The first year was good—sort of."

—MADONNA, on divorce from Sean Penn

"She wanted it. I didn't. . . . I didn't want to lose Sonny and Cher. I was in love with Sonny and Cher. I never saw it coming. It was like a rocket that hit me in the nose."

—SONNY BONO

"I have kept more than a hundred of her letters, many of which are illegible in parts, obscured by her tears. After twenty-five years, I am still filled with emotion when I read them."

—ROGER VADIM, on ex-wife Brigitte Bardot

"Life was good to me. I had a great wife, good kids, money, health—and I'm lonely and bored."

> —O. J. SIMPSON, on ending his 13-year marriage in 1979.
> He remarried in 1984.

"Once Rosey decided her marriage was over, what we had between us blossomed into a very passionate, beautiful love affair. It was as if the barrier was taken down, and we allowed ourselves to reconsider our feelings. That's when we realized that we cared more for each other than just as best friends."

> —TOM ARNOLD, on Roseanne Barr-Arnold

"When my first wife and I divorced, part of the agreement was that I would see a psychiatrist for four sessions, and I agreed. In our first session, I told the doctor, 'I am not the kind of man who can free-associate or look within myself. But I have a proposition: We will alternate between the choice of the topic. You can pick two, and I will pick two. Then, at the end of the four sessions, you will know as much about me as if I had free-associated.' To his credit, the doctor agreed. He was a very intelligent man. One of the subjects he chose for me to analyze was a poem by Yeats. We never did talk about my dreams."

> —HENRY KISSINGER; he divorced Ann Fleischer after a 15-year
> marriage and in 1974, he married Nancy Maginnes,
> a Rockefeller foreign policy staffer.

"It was inevitable that Paulette and I should separate. . . . When I returned home to Beverly Hills she had gone to Mexico to get a divorce. . . . The wrench naturally hurt, for it was hard cleaving eight years' association from one's life."

> —CHARLIE CHAPLIN, on his divorce from Paulette Goddard

"It's amazing what we do to ourselves, how hard it is to grow up, not to fear abandonment, to become a man. It took me a long time. When I met Jayni, it had been five years since my earlier marriage, which lasted all of two minutes. It was hard to get over, because I'd been infatuated with a girl who was so wrong for me. Those were the five years where I really did a job on myself. I was in tremendous pain over that. And then I met Jayni, and for the first time I was awakened emotionally, sexually, and every other way."

—CHEVY CHASE, divorced twice

"I swore I would never get married. I said that for years. My father's marriages were so difficult and painful that I didn't want to have a damn thing to do with marriage, ever. And then I fell in love!"

—KEITH CARRADINE, married in 1982

"People keep asking me if I'll marry again. It's as if when you've had one car crash you want another."

—STEPHANIE BEACHAM, English actress

"Being divorced is like being hit by a Mack truck. If you live through it, you start looking very carefully to the right and to the left."

—JEAN KERR

James Taylor and Carly Simon

Haven't Got Time for the Pain

The Taylors and the Simons were summer families on Martha's Vineyard—where Carly and James got to know one another. They were married in 1972, had two children, and divorced in 1981. Since then, they both seem to have gotten on with their lives. After dating Warren Beatty, Mick Jagger, John Travolta, Kris Kristofferson, Cat Stevens, Al Corley, Keith Hernandez, Albert Finney—all known as Carly's Cadets—she went on to marry writer Jim Hart in 1987. Taylor, a recovering heroin addict, has also moved on in his personal and public life.

As it turned out, James Taylor's heroin addiction was the biggest thorn in the side of their marriage. "I really thought drug addiction was like a virus that he would get rid of. It would run its course and go away. I didn't realize it was an ongoing problem. I thought because he knew the cure, rehab, that it was enough that he was doing it. It seemed to have a simple solution. I was totally naive," Carly said.

When the collaboration between Carly and James unraveled for good in 1981, Carly said, "I was the one who broke down. I said, 'I can't do this anymore.' I initiated the split. But I was also the one who didn't want to see it through. I wanted to get back together. I expected him to clean up and come back. But he didn't. Just as I didn't partake in the drug culture, I stayed very old fashioned in my value systems about marriage. I tried to stop it from happening, but once the ball was rolling ..."

"Baby Sneezes / Mommy Pleases / Daddy Breezes In ..."

Sarah (Sally) was born to James and Carly in 1974, and in 1976, they had son Benjamin. "I can't imagine being in love with my children, as I am, and not having that carry over to the person who created those children," Carly said. "I've never been able to successfully tie off all of those strings. I don't think that they ever necessarily need to be. I find I can coexist with them fine." Carly's sister, Lucy Simon, says, "I don't think that relationship will ever be resolved in her mind." Carly continues, "I have great respect for James, for his art and his role as a father. I don't think I've been emotionally tattered like some ex-spouses who experience bitterness toward their spouses."

As for the effect that the divorce has had on their children, daughter Sally said this: "Some moms don't understand, but my mom really understands me. I can always talk to her—that's why I'll never have to go to a psychiatrist."

Simon Says:

"I dreamt about 'Mockingbird' ... I couldn't tell if it was James and me. Then I realized it was us. Some songs make me sad. But

I never change the station when I hear James." Simon knows all the words to Taylor's songs by heart, even the most recent ones. "Don't forget, I was a fan before I was a wife." "There We Are," a song written by Taylor in 1977, is the only song Simon can think of that James wrote for her. "If I ever hear it on the radio, I'm gone for the day."

Repeat Offenders

Famous Repeat Offenders You Can Count On

	Marriages		Marriages
Muhammad Ali	4	Rita Hayworth	5
Louis Armstrong	6	Barbara Hutton	7
Brigitte Bardot	4	Erica Jong	3
Ingmar Bergman	6	Larry King	6
Milton Berle	4	Hedy Lamarr	6
George Brent	6	Stan Laurel	8
Glen Campbell	4	Alan Jay Lerner	8
Johnny Carson	4	Jerry Lee Lewis	6
Charlie Chaplin	4	Ali MacGraw	3
Joan Collins	4	Norman Mailer	6
Dick Clark	3	Tommy Manville	12
Xavier Cugat	5	Rue McClanahan	6
Bette Davis	4	Henry Miller	5
Doris Day	4	Liza Minelli	3
Zsa Zsa Gabor	8	Mary Tyler Moore	3
Rex Harrison	6	Mike Nichols	3

	Marriages		Marriages
Nick Nolte	3	Telly Savalas	3
Laurence Olivier	3	George C. Scott	5
Christina Onassis	3	Artie Shaw	7
Jennifer O'Neill	6	Frank Sinatra	4
Richard Pryor	5	Gloria Swanson	6
Martha Raye	6	Elizabeth Taylor	8
Jason Robards	4	Lana Turner	7
Ginger Rogers	5	Shelley Winters	3
Kenny Rogers	4	Jane Wyman	5
Mickey Rooney	8	Tammy Wynette	5

"I wanted to be myself."

—RITA HAYWORTH, on divorcing oil promoter/agent Edward Judson

"I can't stand his genius anymore."

—RITA HAYWORTH, on divorcing Orson Welles

"He's a playboy."

—RITA HAYWORTH, on divorcing Aly Kahn

"He hit me."

—RITA HAYWORTH, on divorcing Dick Haymes

"Honey, I've never been without a man in my life! If they think I'm gonna start now, they're out of their heads!"

—RITA HAYWORTH, after divorcing producer James Hill

"On our honeymoon, he threw me out of the car. I never seemed to bring out the best in men."

—BETTE DAVIS, on divorce number three from William Grant Sherry

"I should never have married, but I didn't want to live without a man. Brought up to respect the conventions, love had to end in marriage. I'm afraid it did."

—BETTE DAVIS

"Rather than live with a man for five or six months, we [actresses] get married, suffer for six years and get divorced. It's insane. No more marriages for me."

—BETTE DAVIS, 1989, divorced four times

"I may be stupid, but I'm not mad. I wouldn't marry again if President Kennedy asked me."

—BETTE DAVIS

"It's not my fault when you consider that my three husbands have had 20 wives."

—AVA GARDNER, on her failed marriages to Mickey Rooney, Artie Shaw, and Frank Sinatra

"You have no idea of the people I *didn't* marry."

—ARTIE SHAW, on his seven marriages

"I found the one love of my life three times; the pity is my husbands didn't also find it."

—AVA GARDNER

"In many ways, I haven't changed a bit. I'm still the same self-absorbed guy I was when I married Ava [Gardner]. I like to do what I want when I want, where I want, without much thought for the wants of others. The people around me fare best when they do not challenge me."

—MICKEY ROONEY

"It's confusing. I've had so many wives and so many children I don't know which house to go to first on Christmas."

—MICKEY ROONEY

The record for most monogamous marriages by a female is 22. By a male it is 27.

Well-Groomed

The greatest number of marriages verified in the monogamous world is 27 by the former Baptist minister Mr. Glynn de Moss "Scotty" Wolfe (b. 1908), who first married in 1927. He says he has had 41 children but had only 25 mothers-in-law because he remarried two of his former wives.

Sisterly Love

Scotty Wolfe now plans to divorce his twenty-seventh wife and marry her 15-year-old sister. He had hoped to pay for his new bride's trip from the Philippines with $10,000 he wanted his present wife, 19-year-old Daisy, to earn posing nude for *Playboy*.

"I'm so gullible. I'm so damn gullible. And I am so *sick* of being gullible."

> —LANA TURNER, on her seven marriages

"Artie, she's a nice girl, but it's like sitting in a room with a beautiful vase."

> —JUDY GARLAND, to Artie Shaw on his marriage to Lana Turner, whom he later divorced

Crawford's Dearest

"There was never a doubt in my mind that his talent was greater than mine. I tried very hard to give him more scenes, to build his ego. I dropped by his dressing room to surprise him. I did."

> —JOAN CRAWFORD, on divorcing husband number two, Franchot Tone. Crawford's first husband was Douglas Fairbanks, Jr.

"She's like that old joke about Philadelphia. First prize,
four years with Joan. Second prize, eight."

> —FRANCHOT TONE, on Joan Crawford

"I don't like pauses, and this pause ended in divorce. Never
marry out of loneliness. I owed Phillip an apology from
the first."

> —JOAN CRAWFORD on divorce number three from Phillip Terry

"My sense of right and wrong makes it very difficult for me
to have an affair. I have to be really in love in order to
sleep with a man, and when I'm really in love I want to
be married."

> —LIZ TAYLOR; Taylor was 18 when she married Conrad "Nicky" Hilton.
> After divorcing Hilton, she married actor Michael Wilding,
> Mike Todd, Eddie Fisher, and Richard Burton (twice), then
> U.S. Senator John Warner, with whom she split in 1982. Taylor
> is now on her eighth marriage to Larry Fortensky.

"Liz Taylor's getting married for the eighth time. Her only
regret is that she didn't buy a time-share in Niagara Falls."

> —JOHNNY CARSON

"I was married to a Pisces once."

> —JOHNNY CARSON to Elizabeth Taylor

"I'm sure you were."

> —TAYLOR to Carson

"Happy marriage to me was always what somebody else had."

> —DEBBIE REYNOLDS, divorced from Eddie Fisher and
> shoe mogul Harry Karl

"If I didn't make friends with your ex-husbands and lovers,
who would I talk to?"

> —MIKE TODD, to Evelyn Keyes

Bride Revisited

The greatest number of monogamous marriages by a woman is 22
by Linda Lou Essex of Anderson, Indiana. She has been married to
16 different men since 1957, divorcing the last one in 1991.

Zsa Zsa Gabor's autobiography, *Once Is Not Enough*,
offers vital statistics:
- Number of marriage proposals she's turned down: 4
- Number of sexual proposals she's turned down: 12
- Number of priests she's turned down: 1
- Number of Warren Beatty propositions: 1 (she de-
  clined)
- Number of times she's slept with Frank Sinatra so
  he would move his Cadillac out of her driveway: 1
- Number of pages devoted to her five-year marriage
  to Michael O'Hara: 1
- Number of times diamonds are mentioned: 55

"He vass my virst husband—virst, not vurst. He vass sveet
but I did not like to live in Turkey."

> —ZSA ZSA GABOR, on her first marriage to Burhan Belge,
> press director of the Foreign Ministry of Turkey

"I believe in big families; every woman should have at least
three husbands."

> —ZSA ZSA GABOR, divorced seven times

"You never really know a man until you have divorced him."

> —ZSA ZSA GABOR

"I always say a girl must get married for love—and just keep
on getting married until she finds it."

> —ZSA ZSA GABOR

"Getting divorced just because you don't love a man is
almost as silly as getting married just because you do."

—Zsa Zsa Gabor

"Every woman in Beverly Hills is wondering what to get
her husband for Christmas. Zsa Zsa Gabor is wondering
what husband to get for Christmas."

—Milton Berle

"Marriage is too interesting an experiment to be tried once
or twice."

—Eva Gabor; husband number one was Dr. Eric Drimmer; number
two, Charles Isaacs, millionaire realtor; number three, John E.
Williams, surgeon; number four, Richard Brown; number
five, Frank Jamieson, aeronautics tycoon

"He started to analyze me."

—Paulette Goddard, on divorce from Burgess Meredith. Goddard
wore a necklace made of all her engagement rings.

"You can be the best of friends with a man, and then you
get married and right away he's different."

—Barbara Hutton, oft-married heiress

"I shall never marry again."

—Barbara Hutton, after her divorce from Cary Grant.
She subsequently divorced four times.

"I'll keep trying marriage until I get it right."

—Dyan Cannon, divorced from Cary Grant in 1968
and Stanley Fimberg in 1991

"I've done almost 50 movies—I've had a relationship with
four actresses. They all lasted almost seven years, except my
first marriage [to Judy Carne], which lasted an hour and
a half."

—Burt Reynolds

"I know a lot of people didn't expect our relationship to last—but we've just celebrated our two months' anniversary."

—BRITT EKLAND

"I was never really married anyway. It seems that it didn't exist. I'd take the train on weekends down from Warwick to London and be all worn out, and the next morning he'd be up at six, full of vigor, asking for his cup of tea. I'd say, 'But dear, I'm asleep, you're up. Can't you get your own tea?' The marriage lasted three weeks. Three weekends, to be precise."

—GERMAINE GREER, on divorce from Paul de Feu, *Cosmopolitan*'s (London edition) first nude male centerfold.

"I was never married less than five years to anybody, which proves that there was nothing trivial or temporary about my love affairs."

—ALEXANDER KING, *Mine Enemy Grows Older*

"I don't for the life of me understand why people keep insisting marriage is doomed. All five of mine worked out."

—PETER DE VRIES, *Sauce for the Goose*, 1981

"I've married a few people I shouldn't have, but haven't we all?"

—MAMIE VAN DOREN

"I'm not cynical or frightened about making another commitment. But I'm not eager either. I'm not likely to sit still for long."

—ALI MACGRAW, divorced three times

Down the Aisle for a Little While

	Length of Time Married
Tommy Manville and Sunny Ainsworth	1 day
Rudolph Valentino and Jean Acker	1 day
Buck Owens and Jana Grief	2 days
Dennis Hopper and Michelle Phillips	8 days
Patty Duke and Michael Tell	13 days
Germaine Greer and Paul de Feu	3 weeks
Katharine Hepburn and Ludlow Ogden Smith	3 weeks
Carole Landis and Irving Wheeler	3 weeks
Ethel Merman and Ernest Borgnine	3 weeks
Gig Young and Kim Schmidt	3 weeks
Gloria Swanson and Wallace Beery	3 weeks
Debra Paget and Budd Boetticher	22 days
Leif Erickson and Maggie Hayes	1 month
Burt Lancaster and June Ernst	1 month
Sammy Davis, Jr., and Loray White	2 months
Carole Landis and Willis Hunt, Jr.	2 months
Porfirio Rubirosa and Barbara Hutton	11 weeks
Loni Anderson and first husband	3 months
Michael Bennett and Donna McKechnie	3 months
James Caan and Sheila Ryan	3 months
Diahann Carroll and Freddie Glusman	3 months
Richard Pryor and Flynn Belaise	4 months
James Woods and Sarah Owen	4 months
Ava Gardner and Artie Shaw	7 months
Emmylou Harris and Paul Kennerly	1 year
Barry and Susan Manilow	1 year
Joni and Chuck Mitchell	1 year
Dinah Shore and Maurice Smith	1 year
Suzanne and Bruce Somers	1 year
Loretta Young and Grant Withers	1 year
Ava Gardner and Mickey Rooney	16 months
Marisa Berenson and Jim Randall	18 months

	Length of Time Married
Angela Lansbury and Richard Cromwell	18 months
Rosanna Arquette and James Newton Howard	20 months
Victoria Jackson and Christopher Skinner	20 months
Redd Foxx and Yun Chi Chung	2 years
Kate Jackson and David Greenwald	2 years
Dudley Moore and Suzy Kendall	2 years

Nup Interrupt

During the first minutes between their wedding and the reception, Daniel and Susan Stockwell of Basingstoke, England, decided to get a divorce. He claimed she saw him "talking innocently to an ex-girlfriend and blew her top." She told surprised guests, "It's all over."

When Thomas Mihalko saw his bride dancing with a guest at their wedding reception, he attacked her and tore her dress. The assault charge against him was dismissed at the request of the bride, who said she would seek an annulment of her marriage.

"Beat your wife on the wedding day, and your married life will be happy."

—JAPANESE PROVERB

"A bride received into the home is like a horse that you have just bought: you break her in by constantly mounting her and by continually beating her."

—CHINESE PROVERB

"The trouble with some women is that they get all excited about nothing—and then marry him."

—CHER, divorced twice

"My mother was married eight times.... A lot of my

mother's marriages were when I was too little to remember.
Men were something that you knew were around but you couldn't
quite figure out what their function was. . . . I grew up thinking
of men as these things that you loved against your will."

> —CHER; her mother's eight included three
> separate marriages to Cher's father.

A 1991 study of 17,000 British families found that girls
from divorced families were more likely to become unwed mothers, to marry and have children at a young age
and to get divorced than were comparable girls from in-
tact families.

"Thank heavens I'm not another albatross around his neck.
That is important to me, not to be another drain. He is supporting
two ex-wives."

> —DIXIE CARTER, on Hal Holbrook

"What women look for in a man: Breathing, IQ over 80, weight
under 550 pounds, fewer than six ex-wives. What men look
for in a woman: Pia Zadora as she was ten years ago."

> —C. E. CRIMMINS

"What's amazing is that my exs are friendly with each other.
They all hang out together, and we have Thanksgiving dinner
together. What's really funny is when the three of them
get into a conversation and ask things like, 'When Don
was with you, did he ever . . .' "

> —DON JOHNSON, divorced three times. Johnson's parents
> divorced when he was 11.

Till Death Did They All Part

In 1979, three elderly Cincinnati women, who had been married to the same man at different times during the past six decades, all died within 24 hours of each other. The former wives died in reverse order of their marriages.

"One wife is necessary, a second a luxury, a third wife is a waste, and a fourth is punishment."

—AHMAND IRSHAD

"One wife is enough for any man."

—IBN EZRA

Jack Lemmon: Have you ever been married?
Walter Matthau: Once, but I got rid of her. Now I just lease.
   —*BUDDY, BUDDY,* screenplay by Billy Wilder and I. A. L. Diamond

"When I was asked who I dedicated my book to, I said, 'Alice, my wife, of course.' But I was told it wasn't a good idea because the lead time was too long."

—CALVIN TRILLIN

"Here is my message to everybody out there: If I, after four wretched marriages and a whole lifetime of fucking up people's lives, and having them fuck up my life, could arrive at a marriage as happy and terrific as I've got, *anybody* can do it. Jack the Ripper could do it. Heinrich Himmler could do it. Unlikely as it seems, even human offal like Geraldo Rivera and Morton Downey, Jr., could do it. We're talking here about a man with a face of a dog and a woman with the body of a centipede—they could be happy! If I can be happy, anybody in this universe can be happy."

—HARLAN ELLISON

"I find comfort in the fact that women do not stay married to Hemingway."

—ALEXANDER WOOLLCOTT

"There is little difference between husbands you might as
well keep the first one."
　　　—ADELA ROGERS ST. JOHNS, journalist-author, divorced three times

"Every woman is entitled to a middle husband she can forget."
　　　—ADELA ROGERS ST. JOHNS

"My advice to girls: first, don't smoke—to excess; second,
don't drink—to excess; third, don't marry—to excess."
　　　—MARK TWAIN

"Not long ago, on TV I was discussing the family, and
someone in the audience asked, 'Since your three marriages
were failures, what right do you have to comment on the family?'
Well, I *don't* consider my marriages as failures! It's idiotic to
assume that because a marriage ends, it's failed. . . .
Adultery is *not* a reason for divorce! The only valid one
is the death of a union. Today it's ludicrous to expect that two
people stay connected for their lifetimes."
　　　—MARGARET MEAD

"The more times a man has been married the less faith
he has in the male judgment."
　　　—*REFLECTIONS OF A BACHELOR*

"That's why we've lasted for 30 years. When ratings go
down, one of us gets married."
　　　—JOHNNY CARSON, on Carson's and Ed McMahon's
　　　combined total of seven marriages

"Almost everything you have asked for—with the exception
of a mink coat—I have given you. But you show no
appreciation—only boredom, discontent. You can't bear to remain
home of an evening. If you do it is only to cut your toenails. . . ."
　　　—HENRY MILLER, to his fifth and final wife

"I hate to be a failure. I hate and regret the failure of my

marriages. I would gladly give all my millions for just one
lasting marital success."

—JOHN PAUL GETTY, 1958

"Nobody's gonna marry me now. What good am I? I can't
have kids. I can't cook. I've been divorced three times. Who
would want me? . . . Who?"

—MARILYN MONROE, divorced from Joe DiMaggio and Arthur
  Miller

"I lost more clubs over the wives than the players."

—CASEY STENGEL

Bat-Man

Isbrain Marquez Pacheco, 53, was indicted in March 1992 for the
attempted murder of his wife of three weeks, in East Windsor, New
Jersey. According to police, Pacheco said he beat her with a baseball bat after she refused his demand that she not attend a friend's
baby shower. Said Pacheco, "If I had killed her, I would have no
regret," because he was "offended by what she said to me."

"I never met a man who was able to take care of me. I've
been taken advantage of since I was 20. Men have a tendency
to change when they get married."

—JOAN COLLINS, on divorce from husband number four, Peter
  Holm

"I'd been through the beautiful, extravagant, Wonder Woman,
model-type wife. You get home and say, 'Let's go fishin,'
and they say, 'Huh?' "

—HANK WILLIAMS, JR.

"Many articles written about me have pointed out that although
my theme song is "Stand by Your Man," I have had four
husbands. They insinuate I sing one thing and live another.

Well, maybe I do, but it hasn't been by choice. I would much rather have stood by one man for a lifetime than four in a short time.

"... I made a lot of dumb mistakes, but thank God I finally got it right."

> —TAMMY WYNETTE, four-time divorcée with two #1 hit records, "Stand by Your Man" and "D-I-V-O-R-C-E"

"Here I am only 26 and I've already been married and divorced twice. I sat there in my house and thought this was so disheartening. So I wrote a song for me. It was something very personal to me."

> —TRAVIS TRITT; Tritt's country and western song, "Here's a Quarter, Call Someone Who Cares," is his account of two failed marriages

Tayloring & Altarations

I did, I did, I did, I did, I did, I did, I did, I *do* . . . Elizabeth Taylor Hilton Wilding Todd Fisher Burton Warner Fortensky . . .

I.

"Your heart knows when you meet the right man. There is no doubt that Nicky is the one I want to spend my life with."

> —ELIZABETH TAYLOR, wedding to Conrad "Nicky" Hilton, May 6, 1950

II.

"I just want to be with Michael to be his wife. This is, for me, the beginning of a happy end."

> —ELIZABETH TAYLOR, wedding to Michael Wilding, February 21, 1952

III.

"I have given him my eternal love.... This marriage will last forever. For me it will be third time lucky."
—ELIZABETH TAYLOR, wedding to Mike Todd, February 2, 1957

IV.

"I have never been happier in my life.... We will be on our honeymoon for thirty or forty years."
—ELIZABETH TAYLOR, wedding to Eddie Fisher, May 12, 1959

V.

"I'm so happy you can't believe it.... I love him enough to stand by him, no matter what he might do, and I would wait."
—ELIZABETH TAYLOR, wedding to Richard Burton, March 15, 1964

VI.

"There will be bloody no more marriages or divorces. We are stuck like chicken feathers to tar—for lovely always."
—ELIZABETH TAYLOR, second wedding to Richard Burton, October 10, 1975

VII.

"I don't think of John as Husband Number Seven. He's Number One all the way—the best lover I've ever had.... I want to spend the rest of my life with him and I want to be buried with him."
—ELIZABETH TAYLOR, wedding to John Warner, December 4, 1976

VIII.

He is instinctively one of the smartest men I have ever met.... He is a *real man*.... With God's blessing, this is it, forever."
—ELIZABETH TAYLOR, wedding to Larry Fortensky, October 6, 1991

Taylor-Made Men:

"Every man should have the opportunity of sleeping with Elizabeth Taylor—and at the rate she's going, every man will."

—NICKY HILTON

"Elizabeth was a young woman who had tremendous experience with men. She didn't look ahead too far, the moment was all that mattered. Elizabeth told me that I was her greatest lover...."

—EDDIE FISHER, Taylor's fourth husband

"Elizabeth was the greatest love of my life—until now."
—EDDIE FISHER; Fisher went on to marry and divorce Connie Stevens
and Louisiana beauty queen Terry Richard

"After Elizabeth, I thought marriage was suicide."
—EDDIE FISHER; he left his wife, Debbie Reynolds, for Elizabeth Taylor

"I have been inordinately lucky all my life, but the greatest luck has been Elizabeth. She has turned me into a moral man but not a prig, she is a wildly exciting lover-mistress, she is shy and witty, she is nobody's fool, she is a brilliant actress, she is beautiful beyond the dreams of pornography, she can be arrogant and willful, she can tolerate my impossibilities and drunkenness, she is an ache in the stomach when I am away from her, *and she loves me!* ... And I'll love her till I die."

—RICHARD BURTON; Burton, 36, was married to Sybil, his wife
of nearly 13 years when he and Taylor began
"the most public adultery in the world"

"She has a double chin and an overdeveloped chest and she's rather short in the leg. So I can hardly describe her as the most beautiful creature I've ever seen."

—RICHARD BURTON, on Elizabeth Taylor, c. 1963

"I have to face the fact the Elizabeth may be going to take
off one of these days. I have known it deep down for some
time but have never allowed it to surface. Our quarrel
sounded like the room quarrels one hears from the next door
room in a cheap hotel by two middle-aged people, twenty years
married and bored witless by each other. . . . I behaved in
a way to make a banshee look kind, good and sweet. . . .
Well, I went mad, which ended up with Elizabeth smashing
me around the head with her ringed hands. If any man had
done that, I would have killed him, or any woman either,
but I had sufficient sense to stop myself or I most surely
would have put her in the hospital."

—RICHARD BURTON, divorced four times

"The last six or eight months have been a nightmare. I
created one half and Elizabeth created the other. We grated
on each other to the point of separation. It is of course quite
impossible."

—RICHARD BURTON, from *In the Notebooks, Journals
and Letters of Richard Burton*

"I might run from her for a thousand years and she is still
my baby child. . . . Our love is so furious that we burn each
other out."

—RICHARD BURTON, after his second divorce from
Elizabeth Taylor in 1976

Family Matters

"I began to see an awful lot of children who were screwed up because the parents were screaming all night. I decided it wasn't really great advice to say 'stay together for the children.' "

—ANN LANDERS

52 percent of women
39 percent of men
} think divorce is acceptable in cases where there are young children.

64 percent of women
41 percent of men
} with school-age children think the children were happier after the divorce.

"Ben tells me he misses Dad when he's with me, and he misses me when he's with Dad. There's never a time when he doesn't miss the love of one of us. There's never a time when he can have the love of both parents together."

—CARLY SIMON

"You kid yourself if you think being separated does not have
a traumatic effect on children. They are going to feel that
it is somehow expected that they favor one parent over the
other, and that causes conflict. It doesn't sound like something
I would want to experience if I were a child. I wouldn't want
to experience it as an adult."

> —DUSTIN HOFFMAN, divorced and remarried with
> a total of four children

"I wrote *Megan's Book of Divorce* to explore how funny it
was for a kid to be always missing some article of clothing
or to have one dog at Mommy's and another at Daddy's.
The problems of children caught in a divorce are so full of
humor and pathos."

> —ERICA JONG, divorced three times. Jong's third husband,
> writer Howard Fast, sued to prevent her from
> publishing *Molly's Book of Divorce* with their daughter's
> name in the title. Jong changed the title.

"We would have broken up except for the children. Who
were the children? Well, she and I were."

> —MORT SAHL

9 percent of women ⎱ say children are a cause of di-
4 percent of men ⎰ vorce.

"They're so young. They didn't understand. I tried to explain.
Ivana and I didn't fight, so they didn't see it coming."

> —DONALD TRUMP, on their children

"Herbert Pulitzer provided me with my big moment:
defendant in the most one-sided marital split since Henry VIII
axed Anne Boleyn. She lost her head; I managed to keep mine
but lost everything else—my husband, my home, my so-

called friends, my reputation and most devastatingly of all, my children."

—ROXANNE PULITZER

Deadbeat Dad

The man known as the nation's worst deadbeat dad was sentenced to one and a half years in prison by a judge who said he wanted to send a message that parents must pay their child support. Superior Court Judge Robert Gottsfield also sentenced Gregory Morey, 35, to three years' probation for failing to pay $108,000 in support and interest over a decade to his three children from a previous marriage. Morey topped the national list of fathers delinquent on their child-support payments.

"A guy who doesn't leave his wife and kids provided for, he's a bum."

—HUMPHREY BOGART, divorced

Debtor Dad

In Salem, Oregon, former Baptist minister Joe Lutz withdrew from the U.S. Senate race in January 1992, saying that his "family values" campaign had lost credibility because he had abandoned his wife to marry another woman and was reportedly $2,000 behind in child-support payments.

Jailhouse Pop

Georgia state representative Henrietta Canby went on a hunger strike in February 1992 to protest the arrest of her son, who was jailed for failing to make court-ordered child-support payments.

Pop Is the Weasel

The Oklahoma Department of Human Services began publishing a monthly list of the "worst" excuses received for nonpayment of child support. Among the first winners: (1) "I can't afford to pay child support; I've got to pay my cable TV bill." (2) "We only had sex one time; I couldn't be the father." (3) "I will not allow my ex-wife to get rich on my money" ($25 per week).

324,000 women ⎤ regularly pay to support children
4,001,000 men ⎦ outside their households.

Poster Parents

Posters of the "10 Most Wanted" parents behind in their child-support payments will be displayed in public buildings and published in newspapers throughout Mississippi.

1989 Survey on Child Support:

Women who received full amount—51.4 percent
Women who were awarded no support—42.3 percent
Received less than full amount—23.8 percent
Received nothing—24.8 percent

Trial Shot

A man in court for a child-support hearing shot the presiding judge in May 1992 and was later captured in rural North Dakota. Judge Lawrence Jahnke, 49, was in critical condition undergoing surgery. Police said that Ruben Larson opened fire on Jahnke, a state judge.

Larson later drove to a radio station and dropped off a note saying the shooting was a protest against the hearing.

Bus-Ted

Deadbeat fathers who have avoided child-support payments will soon see their faces plastered on buses and trains if they do not pay up. State officials in Boston have stepped up a campaign to catch the worst delinquents by unveiling a "10 Most Wanted" list of offenders whose faces, physical attributes, and biographical information will appear on posters. Each of the 10 has outstanding warrants for his arrest. The 10 owe their families a total of $250,000. The Massachusetts Bay Transit Authority, which operates buses, subways and trains, will display the posters.

"What scares me about divorce is that my children might put me in a home for unwed mothers."

—TERESSA SKELTON

Nine out of every 10 single-parent families in the United States are mother-child families—a statistic that has remained virtually unchanged for the past 30 years.

Child: "The only good thing about divorce—you get to sleep with your mother."

—CLARE BOOTH LUCE, *The Women*

Two children in five now grow up in divorced families.

"Don't have any children. It makes divorce so much more complicated."

—ALBERT EINSTEIN

"The real killer was when you married the wrong person
but had the right children."

—ANN BEATTIE, *Falling into Place*, 1980

24 percent of family households are headed by a single
mother; 3 percent are headed by a single father.

"Marriages don't last. When I meet a guy, the first question
I ask myself is: 'Is this the man I want my children to spend
their weekends with?' "

—RITA RUDNER

"My wife got the house, the car, the bank account, and if I
marry again and have children, she gets them too."

—WOODY ALLEN, divorced twice

"I couldn't see much point in tying myself down to a
middle-aged woman with four children, even though the woman
was my wife and the children were my own."

—JOSEPH HELLER, *Good as Gold*, 1979

"We never had a good relationship. I wouldn't have stayed
with her no matter what. Fortunately, I've been able to move
on and now I'm with a great lady and things are great. She
came with four kids and so did I, so it's like *The Brady
Bunch* at our house."

—BRUCE JENNER, on divorcing second wife, Linda Thompson

"When I'm seventy, I want to be named in a paternity suit."

—ARTHUR GODFREY

"I have always championed women's rights, but this is a
woman's wrong."

—MARVIN MITCHELSON, palimony lawyer, named in a
paternity suit, 1982

"I've got three sons, one by my first wife, one my second
wife had before we were married, and the one I just got in the
paternity suit."

—AARON PRYOR, junior welterweight champion, 1982

"It was very painful. I remember being asked by someone
from the court, whom I wanted to live with: my mother or
my father? I couldn't answer. I couldn't choose. All my relatives
were worried about me. They kept asking me, 'Are you
okay? Do you need anything?' I was hurting like crazy,
and what I needed was to be left alone."

—EDWARD JAMES OLMOS, on his parents' divorce

"Many [divorced men] complain of feeling like Bozo the
Clown, whose only function is to entertain the children."

—IRA VICTOR, president of Fathers United for Equal Rights
    of New York

"Divorced fathers are forced to recognize that there's no
substitute for being there; or rather, there are only substitutes
for it."

—C. W. SMITH, *Esquire*

"They are the passengers of the future, and we want them
to have a good experience the first time they fly."

—NANCY POND-SMITH, flight attendant, on the increasing number
    of children who are traveling alone between divorced parents,
    The New York Times, 1986

"The main divorce routes are along the heavily traveled
corridor between Boston and Washington in the Northeast and
between nearby cities, such as Houston and Dallas in Texas
and San Francisco and Los Angeles in California."

—ROBERT REINHOLD, on the increasing number of children who
    are traveling alone between divorced parents, *The New York
    Times,* 1986

"As complicated as joint custody is, it allows the delicious contradiction of having children and maintaining the intimacy of life-before-kids."

—DELIA EPHRON, *Funny Sauce*

Lives on the Line

William Saunders took 14 hostages at AT&T's New York City offices because he was distraught over a child-custody fight with his wife, an AT&T employee. Thirteen of them escaped when Saunders gave them—one at a time—permission to leave the room to get a drink of water and they never returned.

> 13,521,000 children under age 18 live with their mothers only.
> 1,808,000 children under age 18 live with their fathers only.

"Certain aspects of my personality were formed in the period beginning when I was 6. My parents went through a very bitter divorce and child-custody battle, and my mother or her parents would abscond with Christopher and Bobby and me, and after that I never seemed to know who I belonged to or what would happen next. . . . We were made wards of the court and put in juvenile hall for three months. I remember feeling very lonely and scared, not knowing what was going on. I guess I was more confused than anything else."

—KEITH CARRADINE; his mother, Sonia Sorel, was the second of John
   Carradine's four wives. After the divorce,
   Keith was raised mostly by his maternal grandmother
   in California.

40 percent of married people say that when couples argue over how to discipline the children, the wife usually wins; 25 percent say the husband usually wins.

A Run for His Money

A court in Maine ruled that four boys should be taken from their father's custody because their "health, welfare, and morals" were in danger. Their father, William Radlely, allegedly ordered them to run in front of cars to fake injuries so that he could collect insurance money. The state intervened after a fifth son died while crossing a street.

"That may sound very familiar to you in America, but in Italy, where we don't have splits in families, it was rather extraordinary."
—FRANCO ZEFFIRELLI; when he was six years old, his parents
were divorced and he was sent to live with his aunt

"Paul and I have never wanted to divorce. We try to work things out. Divorce was really unthinkable when I was growing up in the South in the forties. A woman then, like my mother, was supposed to find her self-fulfillment only through her husband and marriage. There were very definite ideas about how a woman was to live. That's what I was raised to believe. And then, when I was quite young, my parents divorced. It was painful, and after it was over my mother lived through me."
—JOANNE WOODWARD

Women whose parents are divorced are 60 percent more likely to do so than women whose parents stayed together. For men, there's a 23 percent greater likelihood.

"I didn't know what was happening to their relationship. I just knew that my dad was away on one hell of a long movie—for two years."

　　—MIGUEL FERRER; his parents, Jose Ferrer and Rosemary Clooney, married in 1953. Eight years and five children later, they divorced, remarried, and divorced again in 1967.

"I was about five when my parents' marriage began to break up. Since then, I've had a divorce myself and I went back and talked to my parents. I asked them how they could do that, split us up. The answer was that you do what you have to do at the time. After that, my dad met another woman and married her and we moved to Reno. She had five kids of her own. Suddenly it was like—bang, zoom!—there were *eight* kids around. I remember in school we had to draw a picture of our house and family and I ran out of places to put people, I put them on the roof. When he and she split up, I never saw those people again."

　　—TOM HANKS; Hanks and actress Samantha Lewes divorced in 1987

"I was just three and a half when my father left. I remember him as this guy who occasionally came around to visit. . . . My father was a stranger. My sister Kelly and I went to spend the summer with him in Sardinia. He had married for the third time. While there, my father asked Kelly and me to live with them in New York and London. I said, 'Forget it,' but my sister said yes. The whole thing shook up my family and hurt my mom a lot."

　　　　—JAMIE LEE CURTIS; her parents, Tony Curtis and Janet Leigh, divorced in 1962

According to a University of Pennsylvania survey of 1,423 children from divorced families:
23 percent of the fathers had no contact with their children in the last five years. The children who had less paternal contact were doing better behaviorally and academically than those who had more frequent paternal contact.

"I guess you can't help but grow up fast when your parents get divorced. You see situations where your mother goes to get food stamps and she's making fifty dollars too much to get them and she's got four kids to support. You know, a mother with four kids living off meat pies three times a week. There are just certain things in life that you go through and feel. It doesn't have to be this way."

> —TOM CRUISE, on his parents' divorce. Cruise married Nicole Kidman in 1990 following his divorce from actress Mimi Rogers.

"I once saw my father walking along the street with another woman. I was maybe 7 or 8 and I was with a friend, and my friend said, 'Hey, look, there's your father.' And I said, 'No, that's not him; that just looks like him.' I went home and for some reason told my mother about it. Well, she went nuts. She said, 'You're going to tell him this.' I begged her not to make me do it. But when he came back, she insisted: 'Go on. Tell your father what you saw.' So I told him. And he said: 'You didn't see me. You're lying. You're making it up.' I ended up getting it three ways. My mother betrayed me. I betrayed my father. And my father betrayed me. It was so awful it's stayed with me my whole life."

> —NEIL SIMON

"I never saw any arguments. I was completely cut off from my parents. . . . I do remember Mother leaving when she was

going to Italy. . . . I remember her driving down the driveway
because it was a long driveway and I remember her waving,
and it was very sad. I thought she was coming back. . . .
I can remember my father in some sort of discussion telling
me that she wasn't going to come back. It was a tremendous
shock. . . . I remember I had a governess who left at exactly
the same time. I had the feeling that everybody was
leaving."
    —PIA LINDSTROM, on her parents, Ingrid Bergman and Petter Lindstrom's,
        divorce. The name Pia stands for Petter and Ingrid Always.

"My father had fucked up my mother's money and stuff,
but my mother was always so pretty, so perfect. Then when
I was fifteen and she was thirty-nine, her second marriage broke
up and she went into a crisis for the first time since my
father left. I had this idea that I wanted to help get her
over this crisis. It was very frustrating. I didn't want the crisis,
I wanted the graceful mother back. Well, I got her back in
about five years."
                                                —CARRIE FISHER

"After my parents' divorce, my father married actress Paulette
Goddard. They stayed together for nearly 10 years. . . . In 1943
he married Oona O'Neill. He was 54, she was 18. Well,
she was with Dad until the day he died. . . . They had eight
kids together, for God's sake, so they must have been doing
something right."
        —SYDNEY CHAPLIN, on his father, Charlie Chaplin, who divorced
            three times and fathered 10 children by two wives

Act in Fertility

Glovis Arteaga Encinas was arrested after Customs agents said he
carried 5.6 pounds of cocaine strapped to his thighs and lower back
through Miami International Airport. When asked if he had any
property or assets, he said, "I have 60 children . . . from 16 moth-

ers." He has had five wives—officially—and was married for the
first time at the age of 16. At his trial, the U.S. Magistrate said
through an interpreter: "Tell him that we want a copy of his diet."

"I couldn't keep track of all the stepdaddies; there must have
been a dozen or so, 'cause all I had to do was turn my back
and a new pappy would appear ... some of them liked
to beat on Little Louis."

> —Louis Armstrong, on his mother's marriages

> 55 percent of black family households are headed by a
> single mother; 3 percent are headed by a single father.
> 50 percent of black children live with their mothers; 2.5
> percent live with their fathers.

"It's a tremendous betrayal. . . . It's almost like being a bastard
child."

> —Demi Moore, on finding out that her mother was divorced from
> her real father and that she was being raised by a stepfather

Mama's Boy

A Tennessee woman of 43 married her son, 26, in 1978, keeping
secret for six years the fact that she was his mother because she did
not want any other woman to have him. She had given him up for
adoption at age 3, then had formally adopted him (along with her
ex-husband) after the marriage. The son believed that the adoption
was merely a name change. He separated from her immediately
upon learning the facts.

> When they remarry, wives are, on average, 3.7 years younger than their husbands.
> 22 percent of women remarry younger men.
> 61 percent of men remarry younger women.

"When my father was splitting from my mom, he told me: 'Don't ever, ever let me put you in the middle of all this.' It was a very rough time for me."

—MARLA MAPLES

Mum's the Word

The Florida Supreme Court ruled in May 1991 that the right to free expression does not allow a mother to say nasty things about her ex-husband to their kids. The ruling came in the case of *Schutz* v. *Schutz,* a Miami couple who bitterly divorced in 1978. Laurel Schutz, the mother, won custody of the children and fled with them. Richard Schutz, the father, caught up with them five years later, only to find that his two kids hated him.

> A study of 142 divorced fathers ages 22 to 67 showed that half said their ex-wives sabotaged their efforts to maintain a good relationship with their children. As a result, children blame their fathers more than their mothers when a marriage ends.

"Once a female has used the male for procreation, she turns on him and literally devours him."

—CARY GRANT, divorced three times

"[Parenthood] was the only way to hook a wily trout."
—DR. JOYCE BROTHERS, on Warren Beatty's marriage to Annette Bening

"I knew they weren't happy, but as a Bible-fearing girl, I had
to rethink my whole faith. I eventually realized that God was
not going to condemn them for getting a divorce. Still, Dad
was the deacon of our church, and it was very embarrassing
that Stan Maples was leaving his wife. But my mother was
longing for more companionship and my father was buried
in bills. The marriage was killing him."

—MARLA MAPLES

23 percent of Catholic women ⎱ think it is a sin for
32 percent of Catholic men ⎰ married couples to
divorce.

"Pure" Hell

Gary Begley, 45, filed a lawsuit asking $180,000 from the World-
wide Church of God in Los Angeles, claiming damages from the
church's preaching to him over the years to abstain from sex. He
asked $30,000 per year for six years between the time of divorce
until the church finally relented and allowed a divorced man to remarry.

"I am being raped of my reproductive rights.... I don't want
a child of mine in a single-parent situation."
—JUNIOR DAVIS (Davis fought over custody of seven frozen
embryos, fertilized in test tubes in 1988. The original
plan was to implant them in his now-ex-wife Mary Sue
Davis.)

"I am in favor of marriage because I think that marriage
is the only way to procreate children and raise them. I do

not agree with women who have children without a husband. Why should they, if technology today permits us to make love without having children? Unless a woman is very strong, she is not ready for such an experiment."

—HUGH HEFNER

Father of Invention

The wife of Brunswick, Georgia, handyman-inventor Teddie Eli Smith, involved in a custody dispute with him over their 4-year-old daughter, said that the child was conceived with a homemade artificial inseminator Smith rigged up with a bulb syringe and hairspray container. She further said that the device had been stocked with the sperm of Smith's 17-year-old son by a previous marriage. Smith's daughter would thus be his granddaughter, and his current wife would be called his first wife's daughter-in-law.

"The worst time in my life was when I lived in a trailer with three children and a husband who wanted Jell-O every night."

—ROSEANNE BARR-ARNOLD, divorced from Bill Pentland after a 15-year marriage

According to the U.S. Census Bureau report on the characteristics of the American family in 1990: There were 9.7 million single parents in the nation, 41 percent more than 10 years earlier.

"All happy families are like one another; each unhappy family is unhappy in its own way."

—LEO TOLSTOY, *Anna Karenina,* 1877

Look at my family. It's a great group of people. To want more than that requires some pondering."

—TOM HAYDEN, before divorcing Jane Fonda

"Tom brooded about his past and . . . became very raw, very vulnerable, very emotional, in some ways distant. He became convinced that . . . our family would fall apart."

—JANE FONDA, on ex-husband Tom Hayden

The Good-bye Girl

"It was very important for all of us to be a family again. The girls wanted it. I wanted it. Neil wanted it. It turned out he had a lot of mourning to do after we got married. But there was a continuity that allowed the girls to grow up in a good environment, loved by both of us. It is interesting that Neil and I started to have difficulties once the kids were raised and more or less out of the house. Maybe that says something about our time together. Maybe that says what was important about it."

—MARSHA MASON, on marrying Neil Simon four months after his first wife's death

"If I'd known how big Garth was going to become, I don't know if I would have married him. All I've ever wanted was a white picket fence and kids—nothing more, nothing less—and I thought I was marrying the boy next door."

—SANDY BROOKS, wife of country singer Garth Brooks

"Carrie kept waiting for him to come home. He was a big recording star and she'd hear his music on the radio and say 'Daddy? Da-da?' Inside, she never got over it."

—DEBBIE REYNOLDS; Eddie Fisher left her and their two children, Carrie and Todd, for Elizabeth Taylor after an 18-month marriage

"I can confirm that Mick and I are separated and I suppose we'll get a divorce. I'm in too much pain for this to go

on any longer. . . . The day after Georgia was born, Mick left
to go to Thailand. A man is supposed to be with his woman
when she's just had a baby."

> —JERRY HALL; Hall and Mick Jagger married in 1990 after a
> 15-year relationship. The *Daily Mail* said Hall, 34,
> confronted her husband over gossip about his "infatuation"
> with Italian model Carla Bruni, 23, who denied having
> an affair with Jagger, 49. Hall gave birth to Mick
> Jagger's fifth child (his third with her) in 1992.

"The one saving grace for Lisa was that her father was always
there. We have the relationship that we have because she
never felt the worst effects of divorce. He had a house right
down the street from us, and Lisa always had the freedom to
come and go. I'm thankful for that."

> —PRISCILLA PRESLEY

"The man in my hospital room that day was the man I
loved, and will always love. He didn't have to try to be strong
and decisive or sexy, he wasn't afraid to show his warmth or
vulnerability. He didn't have to act the part of Elvis Presley,
superstar. He was just a man, my husband."

> —PRISCILLA PRESLEY, on giving birth to Lisa Marie who was five
> years old when her parents divorced and nine when Elvis
> died

"What should have sealed our happiness in fact forced us
apart. According to romantic tradition, a home and children
are the lifeblood of a marriage. For us, though, they were a
bone of contention, the worm in the apple, the fly in the
ointment."

> —ROGER VADIM, on marriage to Jane Fonda

". . . I was holding Michael's hand. Michael took my other
hand and put it in Diana's and said, 'Now the family is
together.' My heart broke along with Michael's."

> —KIRK DOUGLAS, on Michael's reaction to his parents' divorce

"When we were first divorced, Michael had a lot of anger. He still has a lot of residual anger. It's a warring thing on him ... and it disturbs him."

— DIANA DARRID, Michael Douglas's mother

A 1990 Louis Harris telephone survey of 1,250 adults concluded:
48 percent (representing 85 million adults) said that a happy family was the most essential thing in their lives.
29 percent said a good income was essential.
24 percent said a satisfying sex life was important.

The Final Days: *Carl Bernstein* v. *Nora Ephron*

When *Heartburn* was published to good reviews and best-sellerdom, there was debate as to whether Ephron, the wronged wife, had exploited her children in the process. *Heartburn* is based on Ephron's four-year marriage to Watergate reporter, Carl Bernstein, who cowrote *All the President's Men*. Ephron, 38, was pregnant with their second child when the 35-year-old Bernstein had an affair with Margaret Jay, then the wife of Peter Jay, the British ambassador to Washington. Both Ephron and Bernstein had been divorced once before.

"The end of a marriage is, to some extent, about failure. And failure is not something you like to confront, particularly if—like me or Nora—you're not used to failing. Then, instead of our having the ordinary situation, where you're able to move on rapidly from the point at which you separate, Nora created the single vehicle that could keep us connected, in terms of the destructive aspects of the marriage—which is to say, 'Shit, now we don't have a marriage to fight over; we have a book and a movie to fight over.' It would have been funny if our lives weren't involved and, particularly, the lives of little kids," Bernstein said.

Nora Ephron did not agree with his outrage over her book: "I continue to be perplexed and amazed. To the best of my knowledge, divorce is essentially the main topic of American fiction for the last 30 or 40 years—Updike, Bruce Jay Friedman, Mailer, Philip Roth, etc.," Ephron said. "I have read countless books on divorce, most of them better than mine. The thing that has perplexed me about this issue—do people think that the children are not going to be aware that we aren't living together?"

Shortly after the filming of *Heartburn* began, it was announced in a *Washington Post* story that the Ephron-Bernstein marriage had finally ended in divorce the previous week in DC Superior Court. Bernstein won the right to read the screenplay, "and any subsequent drafts written for the movie, view one of the first cuts of the movie, and submit any concerns." The agreement also set aside a percentage of profits from the film in trust for their children.

"When you give away what you sing to your infant child in the nursery, when you give away a poem that you wrote your wife, you give away your soul! And that's what Nora did," Bernstein said. "You don't go on crap shoots with your children. I don't have any difficulty with a movie about divorce and what it means. . . . If this were only about Nora and me, then there would be no problem.

"Adults can handle themselves. But when peers of our children say, 'Oh, I saw a movie about your mom and dad,' it has this disorienting effect of . . . a great big movie, about a difficult time for their family. . . . If Nora were truly responsible, she wouldn't have sold it to the movies. It has to do with making a large entertainment out of something that can't possibly be beneficial to your children."

Ephron was aware that the movie raised the possibility of causing harm to their children. She also maintained that "Carl was using the children as pawns in a nuisance suit" when he threatened to halt the movie.

"The fact is," Bernstein said, "I'm rather protective about Nora. She's my ex-wife. I try to be protective of her feelings regardless of all this; nonetheless, I'll say some rather strong things about what she did because I think it was reckless and irresponsible. And she worked at it like a dog at a bone. But that doesn't obviate the fact that Nora is a wonderful person, capable of great work. She has truly wonderful qualities, and she is a terrific mother."

Ephron's feelings about their marriage and children were best summarized in 1983 with *Heartburn:* "After Sam was born, I remember thinking that no one had ever told me how much I would love my child; now, of course, I realized something else no one tells you: that a child is a grenade. When you have a baby, you set off an explosion in your marriage, and when the dust settles, your marriage is different from what it was. Not better, necessarily; not worse necessarily; but different."

Of Bernstein's affair with Margaret Jay, he had this to say: "Let me say, unequivocally, that the breakup of my marriage is a consequence of my actions. Absolutely. There is no question about it."

The lesson was not lost on Ephron. In one scene of the movie, the man who plays her father responds to her discontent over her husband's infidelity: "You want monogamy, marry a swan," he said. "I certainly think monogamy is desirable," Bernstein commented. "Clearly, if you're going to be with someone, you want to really be with her, and you can't have a marriage and spend all of your time fucking your brains out. That's not what happened with Nora and me. I think it would surprise a great number of people to know that monogamy was never the basic issue of our marriage. Yes, I did choose to be with someone else. But did I fuck around during our marriage? No."

The Ephron-Bernstein fracas went on for some time, the breakup punctuated with comments like, "Carl is capable of having sex with a Venetian blind," and "he's a piece of work in the sack."

Bernstein on _Heartburn:_

"It's a silly little story about two people who fucked up."

Just Say No to Marriage

"If Congress and President Bush had any guts, they'd crack down and put a stop to the whole mess. We'd have a slogan: 'Just Say No to Marriage.' And we'd have a czar who would go after any wedlock users."

—MIKE ROYKO

"If George Bush reminds many women of their first husbands, Pat Buchanan reminds women why an increasing number of them are staying single."

—JUDY PEARSON, professor of interpersonal relations at Ohio University, on the 1992 Republican presidential candidates

"Politics doesn't make strange bedfellows—marriage does."

—GROUCHO MARX

"I think marriage is a hindrance to love."

—FAYE DUNAWAY

"Love is so much better when you are not married."

—MARIA CALLAS

"Matrimony: I hate it because it is the grave of love."

—CASANOVA

Half-ashed

A Miami, Florida, judge's dilemma: Who should get the cremated remains of Peter Moldenhauer, a former field hockey star? His widow and two daughters from a first marriage fought for the ashes for more than four months. In June 1991, Judge Robert Newman came up with a solution: Each side gets half. Newman ordered a Vienna, Virginia, funeral home to divide the ashes "into two equal parts." One-half will be buried at Arlington in Virginia—according to the wishes of daughters Christina and Gabrielle, who live nearby. The remaining remains will be flown to St. Augustine National Cemetery—per widow Carol Moldenhauer's wishes.

"Music played at weddings always reminds me of the music played for soldiers before they go off to battle."

—HEINE

"Marriage is like life in this—that it is a field of battle, and not a bed of roses."

—ROBERT LOUIS STEVENSON, *Virginibus Puerisque*

"Marriage is an arrangement by which two people start by getting the best out of each other and often end by getting the worst."

—GERALD BRENAN

"Marriage is a custom brought about by women who then proceed to live off men and destroy them, completely enveloping the man in a destructive cocoon or eating them away like a poisonous fungus on a tree."

—RICHARD HARRIS, *Beverly Hills People*

"Marriage is a great institution, but I'm not ready for an institution."

—MAE WEST, divorced once, never remarried

"Marriage is a mistake every man should make."

—GEORGE JESSEL

"Marriage is a good deal like taking a bath—not so hot once you get accustomed to it."

—MORE PLAYBOY PARTY JOKES, 1965

"If marriage hadn't existed as a natural phenomenon I would never have invented it."

—GEORGE BERNARD SHAW; Shaw's parents separated in 1875

"Marriage . . . is not really a natural state. In nature, coupling is almost always for the sole purpose of mating. Few members of the animal kingdom stay together in couples after mating, except for carrier pigeons and whales. Are you going to stay together with one mate because of carrier pigeons and whales?"

—DAN GREENBURG AND SUZANNE O'MALLEY

"The bachelor is a peacock, the engaged man a lion, and the married man a jackass."

—GERMAN PROVERB

"He's a tiger sometimes, he's a lamb sometimes, he's a monkey on occasion, and a fair amount of the time he's a jackass. . . . He's like all men, he's different every day."

—NORRIS CHURCH, Norman Mailer's sixth wife

"I never married because there was no need. I have three pets at home that answer the same purpose as a husband. I have a dog that growls every morning, a parrot that swears all afternoon and a cat that comes home late at night."

—MARIE CORELLI, English novelist, Picking on Men

1.6 percent of women ⎱ who live on farms are di-
4.7 percent of men ⎰ vorced.

"Women are like elephants to me—I like to look at 'em, but
I wouldn't want to own one."

—W. C. FIELDS

"Q: Can you give me an example of a preposterous lie that
tells a great deal about life?
A: Indeed. The vows of Holy Matrimony."

—JOHN CHEEVER, *Paris Review,* 1976

"Why would people want to—unless they had children,
I suppose—why would they want to enter into some lifelong
project? Mix their books together? [Being together] when they
really take each other for granted?"

—JEFF GOLDBLUM, on divorce from actress Geena Davis.
It was the second marriage for both.

She Did It Her Way

Barbara Mossner, 41, of Michigan was ordered to pay her ex-
husband $2,800 for damaging his 400-record collection of Frank
Sinatra albums after the couple's bitter divorce. Mossner's husband
had valued the collection at $80,000.

" 'Tis better to have loved and lost than to be stuck with a
real loser the rest of your entire, miserable existence!"

—HALLMARK CARDS, INC.

"The minute someone wants to marry me, I want to go.

My marriages were so disastrous, I think I'd rather jump off
the Empire State Building."

—CHER

"If I ever marry it will be on sudden impulse, as a man
shoots himself."

—H. L. MENCKEN

Cupid's Arrow

A man distraught over his divorce shot himself fatally in the head
with an arrow from a crossbow on Valentine's Day after chasing
his ex-wife around her house with a knife, police said. Jeffrey Valentine, 32, of Toledo, Ohio, showed up at his ex-wife's house about
3 A.M. She let him in, and he began chasing her with a knife. The
woman's boyfriend got Valentine out of the house and called the
police. Before officers arrived, Valentine took a crossbow from his
car and shot himself in the head.

"The surest way to be alone is to get married."

—GLORIA STEINEM

"Most marriages don't add two people together. They
subtract one from the other."

—IAN FLEMING

"If you want to sacrifice the admiration of many men for the
criticism of one, go ahead, get married."

—KATHARINE HEPBURN

"I really am not crazy about a blood-thick relationship. I just
want to do what I want to do. I might be with her, I might
see another girl I want to date. And I want to be in a
position to do that. . . . I like to have someone to go out
with, to take to dinner. But I'm not looking to be hanging out
with her for twenty years or anything."

—MIKE TYSON, after divorce from Robin Givens

"Being married implies ownership. When you're not
married there's a certain respect and admiration that you'll always
get because no one owns you. . . . So often I see that the guy
goes after the gal and he does everything to catch her, to
charm her—and as soon as that marriage and that piece
of paper exists it's different. . . . I don't ever again want anyone
to own me the way Elvis did."

> —PRISCILLA PRESLEY; she was 16 when Elvis brought her
> to live at Graceland

"Marriage has caused us both a lot of grief. Maybe later on
in life we'll get married. But right now, we're so close to these
ex-spouses who keep knocking on the door. And we look
at each other and I think, 'Gee, I just love you too much
to put that ring on your finger.' "

> —GOLDIE HAWN; she has lived with Kurt Russell for eight years.
> Russell is divorced from actress Season Hubley.

"Oh! How many torments lie in the small circle of a
wedding ring."

> —COLLEY CIBBER, *The Double Gallant*

"If marriages are made in heaven, they should be made
happier."

> —THOMAS SOUTHERNE, *The Fatal Marriage*

"Divorces are made in heaven."

> —OSCAR WILDE; Wilde had a homosexual affair with Lord Alfred
> Douglas and was accused of sodomy by Douglas's father.
> Wilde's wife (Constance Lloyd), sought anonymity after
> the scandal and changed her name. She sent their two children
> to Switzerland and left England and Oscar.

"Marriage is neither heaven nor hell; it is simply purgatory."

> —ABRAHAM LINCOLN

"What is wedlock forced but a hell, / An age of discord and continual strife? Whereas the contrary bringeth bliss / And is a pattern of celestial peace."

—SHAKESPEARE, *Henry VI*

"Though women are angels, yet wedlock's the devil."

—BYRON, *Hours of Idleness to Eliza*

"I've sometimes thought of marrying and then I've thought again."

—NOËL COWARD

Steve Guttenberg: I keep thinking I'll be missing out on things, you know?
Daniel Stern: Yeah, that's what marriage is all about.

—*DINER,* screenplay by Barry Levinson

"Never get married while you're going to college; it's hard to get a start if a prospective employer finds you've already made one mistake."

—K. HUBBARD

"Any intelligent woman who reads the marriage contract, and then goes into it, deserves all the consequences."

—ISADORA DUNCAN

"In order to be happy in wedlock, you must either be a man of genius married to an affectionate and intellectual woman, or, by chance which is not as common as might be supposed, you must both of you be exceedingly stupid."

—BALZAC, *Petty Troubles of Married Life*

"Marriage makes an end of many short follies—being one long stupidity."

—NIETZSCHE

"Love is an ideal thing, marriage a real thing; a confusion
of the real with the ideal never goes unpunished."

—GOETHE

"A certain sort of talent is indispensable for people who would
spend years together and not bore themselves to death."

—ROBERT LOUIS STEVENSON

"Who are happy in marriage? Those with so little imagination
that they cannot picture a better state, and those so shrewd
that they prefer quiet slavery to a hopeless rebellion."

—H. L. MENCKEN, *Prejudices*

"Women have been the slaves of men. Now they're less slavish.
And sometimes to my way of thinking they should be a little
more slavey. Then they'd have more fun. The relationship
would work better if a man could protect and a woman
could do her chore of making him feel great. Someone's got
to make someone feel great."

—KATHARINE HEPBURN, divorced in 1934 from Ludlow Ogden
        Smith, insurance broker/inventor

"It destroys one's nerves to be amiable every day to the same
human being."

—DISRAELI

"If there is any realistic deterrent to marriage, it's trying
to live together afterwards that causes problems."

—SHELLEY WINTERS

"Marriage is a lottery, but you can't tear up your ticket
if you lose."

—F. M. KNOWLES, *A Cheerful Yearbook,* 1966

Not a Lotto Luck

Orange County, California, Superior Court clerks discovered that they had failed to complete the paperwork to make nearly 500 pre-1985 divorce judgments final, thus leaving the parties still legally married. The worst-case scenario for one husband occurred in Phoenix when an appeals court ruled that Bonita Lynch was entitled to one-fourth of his $2.2-million lottery jackpot because the couple was still legally married. Lynch would have been divorced 11 days before the jackpot was announced except for a clerical error that caused the judgment not to be made final.

"The reason most women don't gamble is that their total instinct for gambling is satisfied by marriage."

—GLORIA STEINEM, never married

"Apparently, man can be cured of drugs, drink, gambling, biting his nails, and picking his nose, but not of marrying."

—WILLIAM FAULKNER

"If you can get a good wife, you become happy; if you get a bad one, you become a philosopher."

   —SOCRATES; legend has made Socrates' wife, Xanthippe, the classic shrew, and her name has become synonymous with a quarrelsome, nagging, shrewish wife or woman. In *The Taming of the Shrew* Shakespeare wrote: "Be she as foul as was Florentius' love, / As old as Sibyl, and as curst and shrewd / As Socrates' Xanthippe, or worse, / She moves me not."

"If men knew how women pass the time when they are alone, they'd never marry."

—O. HENRY

"Man and wife, coupled together for the sake of strife."

—CHARLES CHURCHILL, *The Rosciad*

"The only solid and lasting peace between a man and his wife is doubtless a separation."

> —LORD CHESTERFIELD; he fathered an illegitimate son, married
> secretly, and described men as "selfish" and women
> as "frail creatures to be controlled."

"Men marry because they are tired; women because they are curious. Both are disappointed."

> —OSCAR WILDE, *A Woman of No Importance*

"It is so far from being natural for a man and woman to live in a state of marriage, that we find all motives which they have for remaining in that connection, and the restraints which civilised society imposes to prevent separation, are hardly sufficient to keep them together."

> —SAMUEL JOHNSON, quoted in Boswell's *Life of Samuel Johnson,*
> 1772

"A system could not well have been devised more studiously hostile to human happiness than marriage."

> —PERCY BYSSHE SHELLEY; Shelley's father objected to him
> marrying "out of caste." In 1811, when he was 19,
> he eloped with Harriet Westbrook, a merchant's
> daughter. Sir Timothy Shelley reacted by cutting
> off all communication with his son and severing his
> allowance. Shelley and his father never reconciled.

"I could not love thee, dear, so much if I did not love my freedom more."

> —JOHANNES BRAHMS, to Agatha von Siebold upon
> breaking their engagement

"Many a marriage hardly differs from prostitution, except being harder to escape from."

> —BERTRAND RUSSELL

"Marriage is obsolete; a trap for both sexes where, too often,
the man becomes a boss and the woman becomes a shrew."

> —CATHERINE DENEUVE; she bore a child by French film director
> Roger Vadim, between his marriages to Brigitte Bardot
> and Jane Fonda, married and divorced British pop photographer
> David Bailey and gave birth to a daughter by
> Marcello Mastroianni

"It happens as with cages; the birds without despair to get in,
and those within despair of getting out."

> —MONTAIGNE, *Upon Some Verses of Virgil*

"Mine was not a terribly painful, miserable, rotten divorce
with animosity and anxiety. I just knew that my life was going
to have to change and I was determined to make it better. The
divorce was going to improve my life. And it did.

"This may sound terribly selfish, but I love the freedom
that I have. I don't have to worry about anybody but myself.
I don't have to worry about a man's wardrobe, or his relatives,
or his schedule, or his menu, or his allergies. I would not
be married again."

> —ANN LANDERS

"[It is cruel] to chain a man to misery till death. . . . Liberty
of divorce prevents and cures domestic quarrels," and
"preserves liberty and affection. . . . [Divorce] restores to
women their natural right and equality. . . ."

> —THOMAS JEFFERSON; c. 1771 Jefferson prepared notes for the divorce
> case of Dr. James Blair of Williamsburg, who wished to
> divorce his wife after a turbulent 19-month marriage.

"In marriage you are chained, it is an obligation; living with
someone is a mutual agreement that is renegotiated and reendorsed
every day."

> —BRIGITTE BARDOT, divorced three times

"We did a six-year stint on 'not married,' and then suddenly
it was 'Let's fix this relationship,' or 'We might as well be

married.' Then we were married for two years, and it was very on again, off again, as it was for the whole relationship over thirteen years. . . . It got worse because it was supposed to get better. I was supposed to be a better wife."

—CARRIE FISHER, on divorce from Paul Simon

> Ten years after marriage, 53 percent of those who had cohabitated before marriage had divorced; 28 percent of those who had never cohabitated had divorced.

"The divorce will be gayer than the wedding."

—COLETTE, *Cheri*

"One reason people get divorced is that they run out of gift ideas."

—ROBERT BYRNE, author

"In the interest of staying friends, we got a divorce."

—VALERIE HARPER

"We don't elope nowadays, and we don't divorce, except out of kindness."

—JENNIE JEROME CHURCHILL

"You think that single people get ulcers from playing tennis or going skiing? No, 90 percent of the ulcers are married ulcers—from mortgages, commuter rides, yard work, flooded basements, and fighting over why he leaves the toilet lid up and why she calls the bar to see if he left yet."

—MIKE ROYKO

"I belong to Bridegrooms Anonymous. Whenever I feel like getting married, they send over a lady in a housecoat and hair curlers to burn my toast for me."

—DICK MARTIN

> *The Day America Told the Truth,* a book based on an extensive opinion survey, reports:
> Nearly 50 percent of respondents say there is no reason to get married.
> 31 percent of married people are having an affair or have had an affair.
> 47 percent are not sure they would marry the same person if they had to do it all over again.

"Honey, I'm single because I was born that way. I never married because I would have had to give up my favorite hobby—men."
—MAE WEST, 1979

"Thank God for single people. America would never have been discovered if Columbus had been married: "You're going where? With whom? To find what? And I suppose she's giving you those three ships for nothing?"
—RICHARD CHAMBERLAIN

"I'm not going to make the same mistake once."
—WARREN BEATTY; Beatty married Annette Bening in March 1992

I Got You, Babe

For 11 years Sonny and Cher's marital banter entertained millions of Americans. But in 1975, tired of the act and of the marriage, Cher went her own way. Sonny subsequently married four times. As Cher tells it, "I was literally going to jump off a balcony. Sonny and I had been everyone's darling couple. I was afraid of what everyone would think. And when I left Sonny, he said, 'America will hate you.' I said, 'I don't care.' It had gotten to a terrible point. I weighed 90 pounds and I was literally going to jump. I thought, Cher, why don't you just leave instead?"

The Sonny and Cher Show often included the couple's guest star child—Chastity. After their divorce, though, Sonny said, "I think it's a little easier for Chas to be with me than with Cher, because Cher has this high-powered image that doesn't fit into a family scene." Chastity agrees: "One thing I've always liked about being at Dad's is it's always been really calm and normal. That serenity is one thing he gave me that's really important."

Within a year of their divorce, Cher went on to marry rock star Gregg Allman. Of that marriage, Cher said, "I remember one of the worst things that ever happened to me. It was Friday morning, and I was doing the *Cher* show, and I was pregnant and the only one who knew it. My press agent called me up and said, 'Cher, do you know that Gregory's divorcing you?' And I said, without pausing, 'No, hum a few bars.' That's the attitude that gets me through stuff."

Groomstruck

On Cher's time spent with Bono and Allman, she says, "I wish I hadn't stayed with Sonny quite as long as I did. I wish I hadn't stayed with Elijah's father [Allman] as long as I did. I wish I would have cut my losses sooner. Deadweight is deadweight, and a bad choice is a bad choice."

The Beat Goes On

"Maybe I'm not a good person to get married to," Cher says. "I just get tired. Or uninterested. About two years of each."

Marriage Is Murder

"Do I ever think about divorce? Never! Murder? All the time."
—Dr. Joyce Brothers

"It's not that I have any negative views on women. You just kind of have to keep them in place. If that means tossing them in the Dumpster, then that's what you've got to do."
—Morris Day, 1985

A Killer Plot

Evidence introduced in the murder trial of Robert Peter Russell of Alexandria, Virginia, included a computer diskette belonging to him that contained a file called "Murder." Russell was accused of the 1989 murder of his wife, Shirley Russell, a 29-year-old Marine captain whose body has not been found. Among the entries in the "Murder" file were data under the following entries: "How do I kill her?" "What to do with the body," "Make it look as if she left," and "Plastic bags over feet." Russell claimed that the entries were part of a plot of a novel he was writing.

Marital Writes

Adrian Popovici, a University of Montreal law professor and co-author (with his locally well-known lawyer-wife) of the popular newspaper column, "Love and the Law," was arrested after reportedly threatening to kill her.

"My attitude toward men who mess around is simple: If you find 'em, kill 'em."

> —LORETTA LYNN, married at 13 to philandering moonshiner Oliver "Mooney" Lynn, Jr., became a mother within a year and grandmother at 29, still married

> 5.2 percent of murder victims are the killers' wives.

Glad Her Husband Drives a Volvo?

A Houston woman who tried to force her way into a house where she mistakenly thought her husband was having an affair was shot to death by the homeowner. Priscilla Brayboy, 32, and a friend were looking for her husband when they spotted a gray Volvo that looked like his. Brayboy knocked on the door of the house where the car was parked and heard a woman's voice. When she tried to force her way in, a man inside fired at her with a shotgun.

"Homicide is justifiable when committed by the husband upon one taken in the act of adultery with the wife, provided the killing takes place before both parties to the act have separated."

—TASANS

At the End of His Rope

A Cleveland State University anatomy professor pleaded guilty to manslaughter in the death of his wife. According to police, she had been suspended, nude, from a third-floor window of the couple's Cleveland Heights home by a rope tied to her ankle, as preparation for a sex act, when the husband lost control of the rope.

"In any year, more husbands knock off their wives and more wives bump off their husbands than crack dealers zap each other off. And that doesn't count the ones who do it legally. . . . Wives who load up husbands with cholesterol. Husbands who watch TV all night and burp until the woman goes flippo and does a header out the window. Happens all the time."

—MIKE ROYKO

Fatal Food

In 1978 a Paris grocer stabbed his wife to death with a wedge of Parmesan cheese.

Final Meating

In 1984 a New Zealand man killed his wife by stabbing her repeatedly in the stomach with a frozen sausage.

	killed by their spouses
9 percent of wives	} provoke their own deaths
60 percent of husbands	} by being first to use phys-
	ical force or to threaten
	the spouse with a weapon.

Married to the Mob

Baptist minister Ed Lopes was under pressure to resign from his West Richland, Washington, congregation in 1992 following public revelations that he had served time in prison for murdering his second wife and leaving a girlfriend for dead. Although Lopes had not disclosed that information earlier, he had told parishioners that he had done time because he was a former Mafia hit man with 28 notches in his belt, and said the congregation seemed to forgive him for that. Said Lopes, "It's a lot more macho to say you worked for the Mafia than [that] you murdered your wife."

"If you leave a woman, though, you probably ought to shoot her. It would save enough trouble in the end even if they hanged you."

—ERNEST HEMINGWAY, letter to Maxwell Perkins, 1943

Soul Survivor

Chicago missionary Michele Schwartz, 41, was acquitted of murder in the shooting of her husband, the Reverend Charles Jones. The killing happened during an argument over housework and the question of who had saved more souls. When police arrived at the scene, they found Jones dead and Schwartz reading the Bible. At her trial Schwartz said that Jones had beaten her and at one point was "stamping on [her] liver."

Oh Shoot!

M. C. Russell, who was shot more than 20 years earlier during a fight with his wife, died in 1988 from the bullet that lodged in his spine and left him nearly bedridden. Doctors couldn't remove the bullet for fear of causing more spinal damage. The Dallas County, Texas, medical examiner ruled the death a homicide, but investigators closed the case almost immediately because Russell's wife, Lois, whom he had divorced, died in 1984.

"We'll work out the property settlement amicably—with guns and knives."

> —HAROLD ROBBINS; Grace Robbins is ending her nearly 28-year
> marriage to author Harold Robbins. Her decision was
> prompted in part by a May 31, 1991, article
> in the *Los Angeles Times* that said Harold Robbins, 75,
> was seen at the Robbins's Palm Springs home
> with a younger woman.

Twice-a-Round

A woman who shot her first husband to death in 1977 was sentenced to 32 years in prison for trying to hire a hit man to kill her second husband. But the intended victim, Eugene Reedy, said he still loves Bertha Reedy, 47, and pledged to wait for her. She'll be eligible for parole in 15 years.

Home-icide

A winner of Michigan's Homemaker of the Year, who also suffered from multiple sclerosis and was confined to a wheelchair, was charged with murdering her husband with a .22-caliber rifle as he lay in bed.

A Slice of Wife

Fred Apfel, 71, of Colonie, New York, was found innocent by reason of insanity in the 1979 ax slaying of his 71-year-old wife. Apfel said he was driven to kill her because he feared that his $40,000 bank account would be wiped out by inflation and wanted to spare her from the resulting destitution.

Cents-less

A man in a bar in Fontana, California, shot his estranged wife to death on Valentine's Day in 1982 in an argument over an Indian-head penny.

Three Strikes and You're Out

A New York City woman paid two men $20,000 to beat her husband to death with a baseball bat. He survived. She paid the men $150,000 to shoot him. He took about six bullets but survived. Then the hit men charged her another $300,000 for another try, promising this time to get it right. The police arrested all three.

A University of Denver marital studies center reported in 1991 that cities with major league baseball franchises have a divorce rate 25 percent lower than cities without. The center's director said he was not certain what his study signified.

"I felt a mean rage in my feet. It was as if in killing her, the act had been too gentle.... I had an impulse to go up to her and kick her ribs, and grind my heel on her nose, drive the point of my shoe into her temple and kill her again, kill her good this time, kill her right. I stood there shuddering from the power of this desire."
—Croft, in Norman Mailer's *An American Dream,* 1965

Bridge Over Troubled Water

Two days after Kevin Callahan, 32, reportedly stabbed his wife in the throat in St. Petersburg, Florida, and fled, he was found unconscious on a bridge, having been struck by lightning.

2.3 percent of murder victims are the killers' husbands.

Due or Die

At least 1,786 Indian brides were murdered by their husbands or their husbands' families in 1987 because their dowries were found to be too small. It has been illegal to demand a dowry as a condition of marriage in India since 1961.

"Never take a wife till thou hast a house (and a fire) to put her in."

—BENJAMIN FRANKLIN

The Last Laugh

An Albany man who said he strangled his wife under the emotional pressure of a deteriorating marriage has received the maximum sentence for murder. "As difficult as your marriage might have been, you had no right to end it in the fashion that you did," Judge Thomas Keegan told the defendant, Michael Craver. Judge Keegan sentenced Craver to 25 years to life for the 1989 strangulation of Mary Ann Craver. Mr. Craver said he was trying to stop his wife from laughing at him when he strangled her during an argument at their home. He said Mary Ann Craver taunted him about her relationship with another man, a prison inmate, and laughed at him when he cried. Mr. Craver buried her body in a shallow grave near their home.

"Changeable women are more endurable than monotonous ones; they are sometimes murdered but seldom deserted."

—GEORGE BERNARD SHAW

Wed Shock

A Florida assistant attorney general in charge of the criminal division in the early 1980s, George Georgleff, told a reporter that he knew for sure the death penalty is a deterrent to murder because visions of the electric chair once stopped him from continuing to strangle his ex-wife during a domestic dispute: "I found myself choking her, and I saw her eyes start to pop out, and suddenly off to the left or the right, I saw the electric chair."

34 percent of all female homicide victims older than 15 years are killed by their husbands or intimate partners.

The Dirty Dozen

Georgia authorities apprehended Ray Rodgers and his two sons, ages 22 and 21, as they fled Alabama after being released on bond. The three are charged with attempting to kill Rodgers's wife in a 1990 car bombing. According to the Cullman County (Alabama) sheriff, the car bombing was the men's twelfth unsuccessful attempt to kill the woman.

Killing Me Softly

In Phoenix, Arizona, Alfred Lavers, 48, argued unsuccessfully that he should not receive the death penalty for slowly and torturously stabbing his wife and stepdaughter to death. Lavers argued that the law discriminates against poor people who cannot afford expensive guns in order to commit murder and therefore must rely on crude weapons that kill slowly.

22 percent of women ⎱ say physical abuse is a cause of
 4 percent of men   ⎰ divorce.

"John was violent, he drank. It was mostly at night when the kids were in bed. In the morning he would wake up and leave

the house and I wouldn't see him for a couple of days.
We never discussed it."

—JODY WOLCOTT CARSON, Johnny Carson's first of four wives

Brazilian Beat

A state court in Rio de Janeiro defied a Supreme Court ruling by
acquitting João Lopes in the stabbing murder of his unfaithful
spouse on the grounds that he was legitimately defending his
honor. The September 1991 decision drew national attention because it contradicted a March ruling that struck down the "legiti-
mate defense of honor" strategy. The courtroom tactic has resulted
in the acquittal of scores of killer husbands and has drawn fire
from feminists who say it perpetuates Brazilian machismo and
widespread violence against women.

"A man may with impunity kill his wife, mother, daughter,
sister, niece, or cousin on his father's side if he believes her
to be guilty of adultery."

—IRAQI LAW, passed by Iraq's Revolutionary Command
Council, 1990

"If you should take your wife in adultery, you may with impunity
put her to death without trial; but if you should commit
adultery or indecency, she must not presume to lay a finger
on you, nor does the law allow it."

—MARCUS CATO, *On the Dowry,* c. 200 B.C.

"Pleading with him only made him angrier, drove him to
hit me harder, and I willed myself into a Raggedy Ann
doll, hoping to appease his wrath.... My head cracked and
as I went limp he threw me on the bed. 'Now listen, you,'
he said—'you stay there ... and don't move off that bed
... cause so help me I'll kill you.' "

—GLORIA VANDERBILT, on her first ex-husband, Pat Pasquale

Man-Handled

In the seaport town of Horsens in East Jutland, Denmark, they recently opened their first halfway house for battered men. There they provide advice and shelter for husbands whose wives have physically and mentally abused them for years. Svend Aage Jensby, one of the assistants at the center, says Denmark has thousands of men who suffer from domestic violence but are ashamed to discuss the problem. "It's perhaps the major taboo we have today," he says.

No Picnic

Roh Ki-hwa, 34, a Seoul housewife, hanged herself in 1987 because she was embarrassed at her failure to prepare her husband's lunch on schedule during a company picnic. She had forgotten to set her watch ahead one hour for the May 10 changeover to daylight savings time, Korea's first such changeover in 25 years, and was thus one hour late in making the meal.

"Divorce and suicide have many characteristics in common
and one crucial difference: Although both are devastatingly
public admissions of failure, divorce, unlike suicide, has
to be lived through."
—A. ALVAREZ, *Life After Marriage*, 1982

Troubled Waters

Curtis L. Gross, 30, was arrested in Baton Rouge, Louisiana. After allegedly beating his wife, he apparently attempted to commit suicide by locking himself inside the trunk of his car as it was inching forward into a lake, but the car came to rest in shallow water.

Greener Pastors

A Colorado pastor shot his wife, also a minister, to death on a church lawn and ignored witnesses' screams to stop before killing himself. The Reverend Martin Drew, 51, a Catholic priest-turned-Congregational-pastor, had been separated from his wife, the Reverend Regina Kobak Drew, 40. He had filed for divorce.

"Mary and I have been married forty-seven years, and not once have we ever had an argument serious enough to mention the word *divorce* . . . murder, yes, but divorce, never."
—JACK BENNY, 1974

You Don't Bring Me Flour

Walter Davis, 75, was found not guilty by reason of insanity in the 1986 murder of his wife. According to testimony, she had harangued him for five hours one day about a conversation he had had, in her presence, with a woman in a grocery store on how to preserve unused portions of a loaf of bread.

Truth Is Strangler than Fiction

In January 1992, Judge Neil Denison gave an 18-month suspended sentence to Bisla Rajinder Singh in Erith, England, after he had been convicted of strangling his wife to death. The judge explained that Singh had been "nagged" too much by his wife and had stayed with her only to protect the children.

"There are only about 20 murders a year in London and not all are serious—some are just husbands killing their wives."
—G. H. HATHERHILL, Commander, Scotland Yard, 1954

Miss Mannered

A London man was accused of strangling his wife to death because she put a pot of mustard and a newspaper on the wrong side of the plate at dinner.

Lady Astor to Winston Churchill: "If you were my husband, I'd put poison in your coffee."
Winston Churchill to Lady Astor: "If you were my wife, I'd drink it."

Means to an End

A Louisville woman pleaded guilty to adding powerful laxatives to her husband's vitamin capsules every day for three months in order to make him ill so that his family would offer him financial assistance on the couple's overdue mortgage payments.

"When you consider what a chance women have to poison their husbands, it's a wonder there isn't more of it done."
—KIN HUBBARD

Raw Deal

A Parisian night watchman killed his second wife in 1972 because, police theorized, she had overcooked the roast. Seventeen years earlier he had killed his first wife because she had undercooked a meal.

Love Me Slender

A doctor whose wife died as he performed liposuction on her in his office went to trial on a murder charge. Joe Bill Reynolds's wife, Sharon, 43, died during a 4-hour operation in 1989. The liposuction left her with a 2-foot-long wound and drained most of the blood from her body.

> Happily married women gain an average of 18.4 pounds in the first 13 years of marriage, whereas unhappily married women gain an average of 42.6 pounds. On their wedding days, the average weight difference between these women is only 5 pounds.

Domestically **S**peaking

"One time he chased me out of the house in his bathrobe. Another time he threw a bagel and cream cheese all over my dress when I was going to the Met. I'd pull up to the driveway and say, 'Is it safe to come home?' "

> —BRENDA BOOZER, Metropolitan Opera singer, on her divorce from actor Robert Klein

A Striking Blow

A 30-year-old woman was accused by Oakland police of shooting her husband in 1989, after tailing him on a freeway and pulling alongside his car. Police say that the incident started earlier in the evening when the husband rolled a gutter ball while bowling, causing them to lose by six pins to another couple.

Blowing His Stack

Runo Cairenius, 51, retaliating against his wife in a domestic dispute, rigged a cable to a hook embedded in concrete in his backyard and ripped the entire roof off his Brampton, Ontario, house.

"All married couples should learn the art of battle as they should learn the art of making love. Good battle is objective and honest—never vicious or cruel. Good battle is healthy and constructive, and brings to a marriage the principle of equal partnership."

—ANN LANDERS

"The way to handle wives, like the fellow says, is to catch 'em early, treat 'em rough, and tell 'em nothing!"

—NAT HICKS, *Main Street* by Sinclair Lewis, 1920

"A woman, an ass, and a walnut tree, / Bring the more fruit, the more beaten they be."

—ENGLISH PROVERB, sixteenth century

"Women should be struck regularly, like gongs."

—VICTOR, in Noël Coward's *Private Lives,* 1930

Boy Meets Squirrel

A Sacramento man who hit his wife with a frozen squirrel was jailed on suspicion of spousal abuse. Kao Khae Saephan, 26, had been arguing with his wife when he walked into the kitchen and took several frozen squirrels from the freezer and struck the woman, a police spokeswoman said.

"I adore women. I am their total slave up to a certain point. I pamper them, cater to them, but when necessary, you have to bop 'em."

—TELLY SAVALAS, 1975

"Love well, whip well."
            —BENJAMIN FRANKLIN, *Poor Richard's Almanack,* 1733

One More Hit

David Thomas Solomon, 35, at the Clermont, Florida, police station to file charges against his wife for hitting him, allegedly became fixated on a bag of marijuana (confiscated in another case) on Detective Danny Cheatham's desk and, according to Cheatham, "literally begged me for it and stated he wouldn't tell nobody where he got it." Cheatham then set up a hidden microphone in another room, sold the drugs to Solomon there for six bucks, and arrested him.

Second Coat

Lady Sarah Graham-Moon, who is divorcing Sir Peter Graham-Moon after 25 years of marriage, says she dumped paint over her husband's BMW and trimmed 4 inches off the left sleeves of 32 of his suits. She also confessed that she had distributed 70 prime bottles from his wine cellar around the village of East Garston, about 60 miles west of London. Lady Sarah said the divorce was proceeding amicably until she discovered he had moved in with a woman nearby. She said she has instructed her lawyer to halt the divorce proceedings: "I have now stopped the decree absolute until I get everything I want. I don't want him back ... [but] I am not going to be alone and poor. I really think that I dealt with it in a way that suited me, and suited what I thought was the perpetrator of my unhappiness."

Bond of Matrimony

Police in West Plains, Missouri, arrested Sallie Jo Walker, 34, for beating up her husband, Dennis, in the foyer of the West Plains police station in 1991. Sallie had just posted the $200 bond to free Dennis after his arrest for peeping into the windows of the girls' locker room at West Plains High School.

Hounded

In Birmingham, Alabama, a man was convicted of assault and battery after hitting his wife over the head with their 1½ pound chihuahua during a domestic dispute.

Ruffed Up

One morning a Virginia woman found the family dog standing motionless on the stoop. The dog had been stuffed by her ex-husband.

Me-Ouch!

In Los Angeles, a 26-year-old man was sentenced to one month in jail in 1988 for killing his wife's six-week-old kitten by cooking it in a microwave oven because the wife had gone to a movie with a friend.

"Everybody in life has had domestic problems."
—AARON PRYOR, boxer, on being shot by his wife

An Officer, Not a Gentleman

An army officer was sentenced to 23 years of confinement for trying to kill his wife by hitting her with a toilet tank lid. Major David Schneider, 35, also will forfeit all pay and allowances and be dismissed from the Army. He was convicted of attempted murder and two counts of conduct unbecoming an officer. A civilian court in Platte County, Missouri, previously acquitted Schneider in another case involving injury to his wife, Deborah. Schneider was accused of flipping her over a hotel balcony railing. She fell eight floors and survived. Deborah Schneider has since filed for a divorce.

Armed Forces

A woman convicted of first-degree murder and conspiracy in the death of her husband shortly after the Persian Gulf War was sentenced to life plus 10 years in prison. Richard Swanson, 35, was stabbed 65 times in the bedroom of his home in April 1991, a week after he returned from Operation Desert Storm. Testimony indicated that Valerie Swanson hid in the bathroom while her lover, Alan Marcotte, stabbed Swanson. Marcotte, 25, pleaded guilty to murder and conspiracy in December 1991.

"Two dollars will buy all the happiness or all the misery in the world. At least that used to be the price of a marriage license."
—EDDIE CANTOR, *The Way I See It*

In 1991, the cost of a marriage license in Florida increased $10, to $63.50; $30 of the marriage license fee is used to fund domestic-violence centers.

Heavy Petting

A 300-pound woman nearly smothered her husband by sitting on him during a domestic dispute, police said. The man was hospitalized and in critical condition and the woman was in custody but had not been charged. The man had threatened to get a gun during an argument when his wife pushed him to the ground and sat on his head and chest, cutting off his breathing, police captain Joseph Purpero said. The couple's two children helped hold the man, authorities said. The 33-year-old woman called police when her husband stopped breathing. The 40-year-old man had no pulse when officers arrived, and they performed cardiopulmonary resuscitation on him until paramedics got there, Purpero said.

Homeward Bound

Rodney Chavez, estranged from his wife, Brenda, invited her to his home, then handcuffed her, "hog-tied" her by tying her ankles to her wrists, and according to a police officer, "tried to get her to reconcile."

"Marry, and with luck / it may go well. But when a marriage fails, / then those who marry live at home in hell."
—EURIPIDES, *Orestes,* 408 B.C.

Hair-raising

A Brooksville, Florida, man, angered over his wife's new hairdo, tried to kill her by cutting a hole in their water bed and holding her head underwater. His wife's son stopped him by hitting him with a walking stick. The son said that the man had been waving a pistol around their mobile home.

"I had a rough marriage. My wife was an immature woman.
I would be at home taking a bath and my wife would walk
right in whenever she felt like it and sink my boats."

—WOODY ALLEN, on his first marriage

10 percent of women ⎫ think their spouses are a major
7 percent of men   ⎭ cause of stress.

"We faced all the cliché things. We could check all the boxes
in the stress test. His success, my success, buying a house,
building a house. There were never any fights or arguments,
but we didn't seem to be connecting. We just asked each
other, 'Is this it? Are we happy?' I don't think so."

—PENNY MARSHALL, on divorce from Rob Reiner

"More marriages have been ruined by irritating habits than
by unfaithfulness."

—H. R. L. SHEPPARD, American clergyman

A Clean Break

A judge in London, England, granted a divorce to a woman whose
husband, a paper cutter, refused to bathe more than once a week,
never changed clothes, and habitually came home from work with
his ears stuffed with shredded paper.

1 percent of wives   ⎫ never use the washing
27 percent of husbands ⎭ machine.

"I'll tell you the real secret of how to stay married. Keep the cave clean. They want the cave clean and spotless. Air-conditioned, if possible. Sharpen his spear, and stick it in his hand when he goes out in the morning to spear that bear; and when that bear chases him, console him when he comes home at night, and tell him what a big man he is, and then hide the spear so he doesn't fall over it and stab himself."

—JEROME CHODOROV AND JOSEPH FIELDS, *Anniversary Waltz,* 1954

Kangaroo Courting

A survey of 1,500 Australians released on International Women's Day in 1988 revealed that one-fifth of Australian men believe it is acceptable to kick or beat a wife if she disobeys or fails to keep the house clean.

> 4 percent of wives
> 23 percent of husbands } never use the dishwasher.

"Marriage is the best magician there is. In front of your eyes, it can change an exciting, cute little dish into a boring dishwasher."

—RYAN O'NEAL, 1978, divorced and now living with Farrah Fawcett

> 4 percent of wives
> 20 percent of husbands } never use the vacuum cleaner.

"Zsa Zsa Gabor is an expert housekeeper. Every time she gets divorced, she keeps the house."

—HENNY YOUNGMAN

Something in the Way
He Moves Me

Frazer Pahlke sold his family's nine-room house without his wife's knowledge while she and their four children were at an amusement park. When he picked them up at the park, he drove them to a different house and said, "This is where we're going to live." Pahlke said that he sold the home to divest himself of as much property as possible so that he wouldn't have to divide any with his wife when he divorces her.

> 76 percent of women ⎱ watch sports on TV in an aver-
> 91 percent of men ⎰ age week.

Domino's Delivers

In Scranton, Pennsylvania, Sandra Kaushas stabbed her husband Edward five times after he refused to go out for pizza during the first half of a 1985 Miami–New England football play-off game. He told police he had offered to get chicken at halftime, but that didn't satisfy her.

Sports Injuries

In Houston, 37-year-old Delores Douglas was watching a Disney movie on television when her fiancé, Eddie Harris, switched the channel to watch Super Bowl XXIV. Douglas became so upset that she stabbed him in the neck with a barbecue fork. That same day in Jonesboro, Georgia, Mary Helen Holloway shot herself in the head following an argument with her husband, Gary. Rather than report her death right away, he waited until after he had watched the San Francisco's 45-point rout of Denver at his mother-in-law's home, then called the police the next morning. "I can't explain this wild story," said medical examiner–investigator Jim Mabe. "That game was boring."

In households with a television remote control, women control the remote 34 percent of the time. Men control it 55 percent of the time.

Bewitched

When a 28-year-old Philadelphia resident was arrested for murdering his wife in 1981, he explained that she had been practicing witchcraft on him and offered as evidence the fact that he had become inexplicably inspired to watch "boring television shows" such as *Nova* and *Masterpiece Theatre*.

48 percent of women
24 percent of men
} think that when couples argue over what to watch on TV, the husband usually wins.

24 percent of women
38 percent of men
} think the wife usually wins.

"If you don't have control of the TV remote, you ain't nothin'! Two of my divorces were a result of the struggle to see who was going to control the TV remote. I've written a prenuptial agreement: I get the clicker! If we get divorced, she gets the house, all my cars, all my dogs. . . . I get the clicker and the small television."

—LEWIS GRIZZARD

Target Audience

A man accused of killing his wife said he meant only to shoot out the television set. "He had cocked [the gun] and waved it at the TV. It went off, and he saw his wife fall. He saw her lying there and not moving, and he called us," said detective Joe Oubre. Clarence Lewis, 49, of LaPlace, Louisiana, was booked for manslaughter and jailed on $500,000 bond in the November 1991 death of his wife, Sara Lewis, 55.

Walter Matthau (to Jack Lemmon): "I knew a guy, he had heart attacks, so he got a pacemaker. His wife divorced him because she said it interfered with the TV."

—From the movie *Buddy, Buddy,* screenplay by Billy Wilder and I. A. L. Diamond

News *Dead*lines

A man called Miami TV reporter Art Carlson with a "news tip"—that he had just killed his wife. Then the caller asked if he could be paid, as per the station's policy, for the tip. At first Carlson thought it was a hoax, but police found the wife's body a short time later.

"If I was still married to Jerry, I'd probably be dead by now."

—MYRA LEWIS, on ex-husband Jerry Lee Lewis

"Sometimes I wonder if men and women really suit each

other. Perhaps they should live next door and just visit now
and then."

—KATHARINE HEPBURN

"I think husbands and wives should live in separate houses.
If there's enough money, the children should live in a third."

—CLORIS LEACHMAN, divorced from producer George Englund

"I am happy being single, but I never say I will never marry
again. If I did marry, my husband would have to live next
door or across the street because I could never live with
someone again. I enjoy my place too much to want to give
it up."

—CAROL BURNETT, divorced twice

"We sleep in separate rooms, we have dinner apart, we take
separate vacations—we're doing everything we can to keep
our marriage together."

—RODNEY DANGERFIELD

"If married couples did not live together, happy marriages
would be more frequent."

—NIETZSCHE, *Human, All Too Human*, 1878

"My wife and I tried to breakfast together, but we had to
stop or our marriage would have been wrecked."

—WINSTON CHURCHILL

"We get along. We are tremendously attracted to each other.
We just can't stand living together."

—BRIGITTE NIELSEN, after receiving a $6 million settlement
from Sylvester Stallone

"Our 18-month trial separation had gone so well we decided
to make it permanent."

—JOHN CLEESE, on divorce from second wife, Barbara Trentham

"Although I had grown fond of Mildred, we were irreconcilably mismatched. Her character was not mean, but exasperatingly feline. I could never reach her mind. It was cluttered with pink-ribboned foolishness. She seemed in a dither, looking always for other horizons. After we had married a year, a child was born but lived only three days. This began the withering of our marriage. Although we lived in the same house, we seldom saw each other, for she was as much occupied at her studio as I was at mine. It became a sad house. . . ."

> —CHARLIE CHAPLIN, on ex-wife Mildred Harris. They were married in 1918 and divorced two years later. Chaplin then married and divorced Lita Grey and Paulette Goddard. He was then named in a paternity suit and ordered to support Joan Berry's child. In 1943, at the age of 54, he married 18-year-old Oona O'Neill and they had eight children.

Midnight Movers

A company whose name translates to "Transport Service for Troubled People" in Osaka, Japan, specializes in after-dark moves for wives who want to leave their husbands without alerting the neighbors and before their husbands come home from late-night dinners.

> Japanese women have initiated 70 percent of the 155,000 divorces filed annually during the past 10 years. There were none at all until the end of World War II, before which only men could dissolve a marriage.

The Contender: Marlon Brando

In 1955, Marlon Brando began his tempestuous relationship with Anna Kashfi. At the time, he said, "She's everything I desire in a woman." When she became pregnant, Brando admitted they should be married even though they argued continuously. She accused him—wrongly—of having an affair with French actor-director Christian Marquand and was furious when he insisted on naming their son Christian. Kashfi added the name Devi and thereafter never addressed the boy by his first name.

Affairs with actresses France Nuyen and Pina Pellicer caused Kashfi to sue Brando for divorce, and the ensuing custody battle over Christian was brutal. Kashfi swore in court that on one occasion Brando struck her and threw her to the living-room floor, thrust a carving knife in her hand, and ordered her to kill him. When she screamed that he wasn't worth going to the gas chamber for, he battered her again, slamming her against the kitchen wall. After the divorce Brando took off to Mexico and married Movita, with whom he had a son and a daughter.

Soon after, Kashfi was found in her house, near death from a self-administered drug dose. In the room with her was 6-year-old Christian—crying, hungry, and afraid. Brando received temporary custody of his son and took him to his sister's house.

Further upheavals in Brando's personal life disrupted the filming of *Last Tango in Paris*. Kashfi kidnapped Christian, whisking him off to a tent camp in Baja California. He was found there, frightened, suffering from bronchitis, and surrounded by aging former hippies. At the same time, Movita, whom he had recently divorced, charged him with failing to supply child support.

Brando, who's been called "a gob in the yeast of creation," "a walking erection," and "a total hormone factory," himself once said, ". . . All I want to do is screw girls, eat hamburgers, and drink raw eggs."

Divorced three times with a total of four children, Brando has said, "I have loved a lot in my life. I like love. Nor does it matter that with every woman my relationships have ended up in nothing. I've faced love every time as a necessary good or a necessary evil."

Battle of the Sexes

"Nobody will ever win the battle of the sexes. There's too much fraternizing with the enemy."
> —HENRY KISSINGER; he divorced Ann Fleischer in 1964 and married Nancy Maginnes in 1974.

"The war between the sexes is the only one in which both sides regularly sleep with the enemy."
> —QUENTIN CRISP

"The word *love* has by no means the same sense for both sexes, and this is one cause of the serious misunderstandings that divide them."
> —SIMONE DE BEAUVOIR

"There will always be a battle between the sexes because men and women want different things. Men want women and women want men."
> —GEORGE BURNS

"Throughout history, females have picked providers for mates. Males pick anything."
> —MARGARET MEAD, 1977, divorced three times

"At best, marriage is not an institution that favors women.
Its major transactions are always at the male's convenience.
Whether we stay home or whether we have jobs, it remains
a given even today that the kids, the house and making one's
husband comfortable are basically all our responsibilities."

—MEREDITH BAXTER-BIRNEY, divorced twice

"I think men and women have a sort of obligation between
them to make life attractive and picturesque. . . . I mean, I can
carry the logs up from the cellar and build the fire. I do
all that. But if I were married to someone, and did it, and
he was sitting reading the paper, I would like him to feel that
he's a lazy son of a bitch."

—KATHARINE HEPBURN, 1990

"Before marriage a man declares that he would lay down
his life to serve you; after marriage, he won't even lay down
his newspaper to talk to you."

—HELEN ROWLAND, *Reflections of a Bachelor Girl*

In 40 percent of households the woman usually apolo-
gizes first.
In 60 percent the man does.

"Whenever a husband and wife begin to discuss their marriage,
they are giving evidence at an inquest."

—H. L. MENCKEN

"When a woman wants a divorce, she will search for any
excuse. If the marriage fails, the woman feels guiltier than the
man . . . so she shouts to the world, 'It is because of my partner,
that monster, that the marriage has failed.' "

—RICHARD HARRIS; he divorced Elizabeth Rees-Williams,
who later married Rex Harrison

"When two people who are intimate begin separating, each
one may pretend to leave the other before the other one
leaves the one who is leaving."

—JILL JOHNSTON, *Village Voice*, 1979

"When two people marry they become in the eyes of the law
one person, and that person is the husband!"

—SHANA ALEXANDER

"The only thing that holds a marriage together is the husband
bein' big enough to step back and see where his wife went
wrong."

—ARCHIE BUNKER

"By marriage, the husband and wife are one person in law;
that is, the very being or legal existence of the woman is suspended
during the marriage. . . ."

—SIR WILLIAM BLACKSTONE, *Commentaries on the Laws of
England,* 1765

"At some brighter period, when the world should have grown
ripe for it, in Heaven's own time, a new truth would be
revealed, in order to establish the whole relation between
man and woman on a surer ground of mutual happiness."

—*THE SCARLET LETTER*, 1850; Nathaniel Hawthorne described throngs
of distressed women who came to an older and wiser Hester
Prynne for advice on how to achieve the ideal and happy
marriage

"They say there's discrimination, so they revoke laws banning
women from being truckers, construction workers, or
miners. . . . Who wants to go home to a wife who smells
of cement and has big muscles? [My wife] pilots the stove
rather than a truck. That's more appropriate."

—LUIZ CARLOS JACARE LADEIRA, 1992, founding member of the
Brazilian Macho Movement

"With the education and elevation of women we shall have

a mighty sundering of the unholy ties that hold men and women together who loathe and despise each other."

—ELIZABETH CADY STANTON, woman's rights advocate, supporter of divorce, 1860

> 51 percent of women ⎱ think the women's movement
> 55 percent of men ⎰ has made things more difficult for men at home.

A study of househusbands conducted by Germany's Hamburg Institute for Marriage and the Family Research concludes that liberated men who stay home "are overworked at home and not respected by their wives." Divorce results in 9 out of 10 cases. Marriages between working women and housebound men last on average only four years, said the survey.

"I find now that women have achieved some power and recognition they are quite the equal of men in every stupidity and vice and misjudgment that we've exercised through history. . . . I used to think—this is sexism in a way, I'll grant it—that women were better than men. Now I realize no, they're not any better."

—NORMAN MAILER, 1991

"I am convinced that, even without restrictions, there still would have been no female Pascal, Milton or Kant. . . . If civilization had been left in female hands, we would still be living in grass huts."

—CAMILLE PAGLIA, writer

3 percent of women⎱ say women's lib is a cause of di-
15 percent of men   ⎰ vorce.

"Women want a family life that glitters and is stable. They
don't want some lump spouse watching ice hockey in the late
hours of his eighteenth beer. They want a family that is
so much fun and is so smart that they look forward to
Thanksgiving rather than regarding it with a shudder. That's
the glitter part. The stable part is, obviously, they don't want
to be one bead on a long necklace of wives. They want,
just like men, fun, love, fame, money and power. And equal
pay for equal work."

—CAROLYN SEE

"How much fame, money, and power does a woman have
to achieve on her own before you can punch her in the
face?"

—P. J. O'ROURKE

"Every husband may beat his wife when she disobeys his
commands, or when she curses him, or contradicts him—
provided he do it moderately, and not to the extent of causing
her death."

—PHILIPPE DE BEAUMANOIR, *Customs of the People of Beauvais,*
     c. 1285

4 percent of married women⎱ sometimes argue with
8 percent of married men   ⎰ their spouses about the
                             attention they pay each
                             other.

"The way to fight a woman is with your hat. Grab it and run."

—JOHN BARRYMORE

"A man never knows how to say good-bye; a woman never knows when to say it."

—HELEN ROWLAND

"The great trick with a woman is to get rid of her while she thinks she's rid of you."

—SOREN KIERKEGAARD

"Being a husband is a whole-time job. That is why so many husbands fail. They cannot give their entire attention to it."

—ARNOLD BENNETT

"A woman in love forgets herself, her own interests. All she is thinking of is the man she loves, what she means to him, how she can make him happy. She simply lives to fit his needs."

—INGRID BERGMAN, divorced twice

"Women are here to serve men. Look at them, they got to squat to piss. Hell, that proves it."

—LARRY FLYNT, American publisher, 1976

For every 1,000 married women, 156 are divorced.

"You could put everything I've learned about men on the head of a pin and still have room left for the Lord's Prayer."

—CHER

"I would guess that most men who understand women at all feel hostility toward them. At their worst, women are low, sloppy beasts."

—NORMAN MAILER

For every 1,000 married men, 110 are divorced.

"After a few years of marriage a man and his wife are apt
to be, if nothing else, at least the sort of enemies who respect
each other."

—DON MARQUIS

"Men and women, women and men. It will never work."

—ERICA JONG, divorced three times

Stormin' Norman Mailer

"The fact is that there isn't anything more pleasant than a good
marriage, nor anything less pleasant than a bad one. And when
the meanness that feeds the good as well as the bad marriage
takes over, then the marriage blows up. Mine have all blown
up."

— NORMAN MAILER

Mailer left his first wife, stabbed his second wife with a penknife,
then left wives three and four, fathering a total of eight children—
the last out of wedlock with girlfriend Norris Church. But when his
divorce from fourth wife Beverly Bently came through, he did not
marry Church. Instead, he wed Carol Stevens, a jazz singer who
bore him a daughter before he and Church became friends. After a
"civilized" divorce, Mailer—who said he wanted to give his
daughter by Stevens parents who at some point were married—
made arrangements for his sixth marriage to Norris Church.

The Fight

Mailer went to a party one night, drank much, and became aggres-
sive. He had an argument in the street with the guest of honor and

when he returned home that night he plunged a knife into his wife twice, close to the heart. He missed by sheer chance and then he wrote a poem:

> So long
>   as
>   you
>   use
>   a knife,
>   there's
>   some
>   love
>   left.

(Poem quoted in *The Egotists* by Oriani Fallaci, April 1967)

The Naked and the Bed

"Sex for us [Americans] is like a sport, a competition; the first thing a woman asks about a man is: 'Is he good at it?' So a man when he is with a woman thinks only about being good at it. Everytime I go with a woman, I feel as if I have to defend my reputation: a pleasant but average performance would mean being disgraced in front of the whole city. We make love waving the flag, always concerned with being supermen—which is another reason, I think, for burrowing into family life. Not because of religion or morality but because of health. A bachelor in America must be something of a sex fiend. For instance, I would be forced to throw everything into the great cauldron of sex. But isn't it ridiculous to let the best part of you drain out of your head? Actually, it's a weakness—the least forgivable weakness."

—NORMAN MAILER

Loved Again?

". . . American women believe that they must be equal with men; independence is more important to them than dedication. . . . I once wrote that there is little honor left in American life, and that this lack breeds a tendency to destroy the masculinity of American men, to make them more feminine. . . . Too many men in this country have lost or are losing their masculinity. . . . America is still the most unpredictable nation history has ever produced. Everything can happen here. Even the miracle of becoming loved again."

—Norman Mailer, 1967

The Definitive Divorce

"Divorce is defeat."

—LUCILLE BALL

"Each divorce is the death of a small civilization."

—PAT CONROY

"Love, the quest; marriage, the conquest; divorce, the inquest."
—HELEN ROWLAND, *Reflections of a Bachelor Girl,* 1903

"Courtship is a republic; marriage, a monarchy; divorce,
a soviet."

—HELEN ROWLAND, *The Book of Diversion,* 1925

"There are four stages to a marriage. First there's the affair,
then the marriage, then the children and finally the fourth
stage, without which you cannot know a woman, the
divorce."

—NORMAN MAILER

"It is seldom indeed that one parts on good terms, because
if one were on good terms one would not part."

PROUST, *The Fugitive*

"Divorce is an institution only a few weeks later in origin than
marriage."

—VOLTAIRE

"It is not marriage that fails; it is people that fail. All that marriage
does is to show people up."

—HARRY EMERSON FOSDICK, American clergyman

"What therefore God hath joined together, let no man put
asunder."

—MATTHEW 19:6

"What God hath joined together no man shall put asunder:
God will take care of that."

—GEORGE BERNARD SHAW, *Getting Married*

"Whom God has put asunder, why should man put together?"

—EMERSON

"Wedding, n. A ceremony at which two persons undertake
to become one, one undertakes to become nothing and nothing
undertakes to become supportable."

—AMBROSE BIERCE

Divorce: "Fission after fusion."

—RITA MAE BROWN

"I Do ... I Do"

"In Biblical times, a man could have as many wives as he could afford. Just like today."

—Abigail Van Buren

"I prefer the word *homemaker,* because *housewife* always implies that there may be a wife someplace else."

—Bella Abzug

Courtships

Multnomah County District Judge Robert Kirkman, who admitted being married to two women at the same time and forging a divorce decree, was suspended by the Oregon Supreme Court.

"Bigamy is one way of avoiding the painful publicity of divorce and the expense of alimony."

—Oliver Herford

"I have been called a monster. But I am not. No bigamist

is. Nor yet a woman hater. The man who marries just once
proves only his ignorance of women. The man who marries
many times proves, in spite of his disillusionments, his faith
in women. . . ."

—Don Marquis, *The New York Herald*

Bi the Way

Albert Ducharme, 58, was convicted of bigamy in Winnipeg after
police discovered his wives when they called to rescue him (a double amputee) from his bathroom. He explained that his wife of 16
years, Geraldine, had threatened to leave him unless he also married her lesbian lover, Mary-Lou, so that Geraldine could be "a
wife for me and a husband for [Mary-Lou]."

"Bigamy is having one husband too many. Monogamy is the
same."

—Erica Jong, divorced three times

Tri Again

A woman charged with bigamy in Brooksville, Florida, was sentenced to 60 days in jail and ordered to divorce at least two of her
three husbands.

"If I want to spend Friday evening at his house, I make an
appointment. If he's already booked, I either request another
night or, if my schedule is inflexible, I talk to the other
wife and we work out an arrangement. One thing we've
all learned is that there's always another night."

—Elizabeth Joseph, Big Water, Utah, lawyer whose
polygamist husband has nine wives

Fatal **D**istraction

"There is a peculiar burning odor in the room, like explosives
. . . the kitchen fills with smoke and the hot, sweet, ashy smell
of scorched cookies. The war has begun."
> —ALISON LURIE, on a wife's discovery of her husband's infidelity,
> *The War Between the Tates*, 1974

"As we all know from witnessing the consuming jealousy of
husbands who are never faithful, people do not confine
themselves to the emotions to which they are entitled."
> —QUENTIN CRISP

Snake, Rattle & Roll

Reverend Glen Summerford was convicted in 1992 of attempted
murder of his wife in Scottsboro, Alabama. A jury found that he
had forced his wife to stick her hand into a cage of rattlesnakes
(which he handles in his services at his Church of Jesus with Following Signs), saying that she had to die because he wanted to
marry another woman.

"How can a man who has committed adultery and left his wife and children, be Christ?"

> —EVELYN MANDELA, Nelson's first wife of 14 years. They divorced in 1957.

Rock-a-Bye Lady

The woman who revealed she'd had an affair with the archbishop of Atlanta, leading to his resignation, broke months of silence on the relationship, saying she fell in love with him after he seduced her with nursery rhymes. Vicki Long said she went to then-Archbishop Eugene Marino's home in 1988 to discuss her paternity suit against a Columbus priest. He "started off singing nursery rhymes to me, and then he lay down beside me," she said, adding that he took advantage of her but that "I fell in love with him eventually." Marino, once the nation's highest-ranking black Roman Catholic, has been in seclusion since the revelation of their two-year affair.

64 percent of the wives
28 percent of the husbands } of an unfaithful spouse know about the infidelity.

"Ted's a considerate person, especially to women."

> —JOAN KENNEDY, on Teddy Kennedy

"There were always girls. He never stopped. It was absolutely pathological."

> —DOROTHY HART HEARST, on ex-husband William S. Paley

"Mick screws many, but has few affairs. All my friends slept with him. Monogamy should be honored by both partners if it's important to one."

> —BIANCA JAGGER, on ex-husband Mick Jagger

84 percent of wives } think it is important that
75 percent of husbands } they be monogamous.

"I was pretty good with her."
—SONNY BONO, on being faithful to wife number three

"I cheated on them all."
—GERALDO RIVERA, divorced three times

"He's obviously a scumbag, because he started making love
to other people and betraying my daughter and her innocence
from the very beginning. If I see Gerry, I'll spit in his face."
—KURT VONNEGUT; his daughter, Edith, is one of
Geraldo Rivera's ex-wives

Chopped Stick

Bangkae, Thailand, police arrested an 18-year-old woman, charging her with cutting off her husband's penis while he slept, in retaliation of an extramarital affair. After a neighbor had brought the screaming man to the hospital, the doctor advised him to return and find the penis, which the wife had tossed out the window. The neighbor returned just in time to retrieve it from a covey of ducks.

"Once again, I had let my dick lead away from a carefully
constructed and contented life."
—GERALDO RIVERA, after cheating on his fourth-wife-to-be,
from *Exposing Myself*, 1991

"After a life of promiscuity and a notoriously short attention
span, I was feeling an uncontrolled tingle toward my wife.

It was more than passion or affection. It was more like religion."

> —GERALDO RIVERA, on why he would never again cheat
> on his fourth wife, C. C. Dyer

"Last week Geraldo did a show on female prostitution, then a show on women who cheat on their husbands, then a show on nymphomaniacs. At the end of each one the announcer said, 'Guests of the *Geraldo* show stay at Geraldo's house.' "

> —JAY LENO

A Census Affair

The U.S. Census Bureau office in Pembroke Pines, Florida, received a call from a woman uncertain whether to list as a "third person" in the house the woman whom her husband had run off with and who was now back, cohabitating with him in the couple's house.

"The chain of wedlock is so heavy that it takes two to carry it—sometimes three."

> —ALEXANDRE DUMAS

"[Maggie] has total freedom—and I want it, too. There's no ownership in this marriage. No one can own me. Mag knows this."

> —CLINT EASTWOOD, on his affair with Sondra Locke while he was
> married to Maggie Johnson. They divorced after a
> 31-year marriage.

Case Closed

A California woman was awarded $6 million by a jury in 1987 from her ex-husband, a gynecologist. He and an associate were found to have sewn shut her vagina (during an intended hysterectomy) because he was angry that his wife had had an affair. The two doctors testified at the trial that any mistakes they had made in the 1984 operation were "not intentional."

"Open marriage is nature's way of telling you you need a divorce."
—MARSHALL BRICKMAN

"I haven't known any open marriages, though quite a few have been ajar."
—ZSA ZSA GABOR

"Love will never be ideal until man recovers from the illusion that he can be just a little bit faithful or a little bit married."
—HELEN ROWLAND

"I had absolutely no idea.... That was quite a bomb for him to drop on me between the soup and salad."
—ANN LANDERS; Jules Lederer, her husband of 36 years, told her over dinner in 1974 that he was having an affair with a 28-year-old nurse whom he'd met at his doctor's office in London. He had been keeping her in a second home that he and Ann bought in England.

"To catch a husband is an art; to hold him is a job."
—MAE WEST

"Business indeed. Monkey business."
—FRANCINE DE LA MOUSSAYE, describing the relationship between her husband, race-car driver Jean de la Moussaye, and Roxanne Pulitzer. De la Moussaye advertised Pulitzer's novel Twins, on the front of his car in the November 1990 Grand Prix. He then filed for divorce.

"He's a house guy ... he comes home. I just know that there is only one in his life and it's me."
—MARIANA SIMIONESCU, during husband Bjorn Borg's mid-life crisis at 25. They divorced soon after.

"The prerequisite for a good marriage is the license to be unfaithful."

—CARL JUNG

"All adultery can do is save your marriage. It can't work miracles."

—RUSSELL BAKER

"A gentleman doesn't divorce his wife, even for adultery."

—DORIS DUKE, tobacco heiress, divorced from onetime minister to Canada, James Cromwell

"There is one thing I would break up over, and that is if she caught me with another woman. I won't stand for that."

—STEVE MARTIN

4 percent of women ⎱ say their own infidelity is a cause
6 percent of men ⎰ of divorce.

"Divorce is the sacrament of adultery."

—JEAN FRANÇOIS GUICHARD, *Maximes*

"Adultery is the application of democracy to love."

—H. L. MENCKEN

"Americans are great risk takers. The French think they have it together because a married Frenchwoman in her fifties can take a lover without having it ruin the marriage. The French chide us: 'You Americans all get divorced because you make such a big deal out of infidelity.' "

—ORSON BEAN

"A man can have two, maybe three love affairs while he's married. After that he's cheating."

—YVES MONTAND

| 3 percent of wives | } | who have been unfaithful have had more than 20 lovers. |
| 7 percent of husbands | | |

"It may be possible to find some women who have never had an affair of the heart, but it would be rare to find any who have had only one."

—LA ROCHEFOUCAULD, *Maximes*, 1665

"Marriage is a tyranny, a mortification of man's natural instincts. Man needs a multiplicity of relationships."

—FEDERICO FELLINI

"In our part of the world where monogamy is the rule, to marry means to halve one's rights and double one's duties."

—SCHOPENHAUER

"In Europe, extramarital affairs are considered a sign of good health, a feat."

—JEAN-PIERRE DETREMERIE, Belgian legislator

"Eighty percent of married men cheat in America. The rest cheat in Europe."

—JACKIE MASON

"I wanted Petter to know I was leaving him, that I was unfaithful. So I wrote that letter to Petter telling the truth: 'I have found the place where I want to live, these are my people, and I want to stay here and I'm sorry. . . .' I felt that I was free. That was my divorce. I had been honest. . . . There were so many years when I was just waiting to find somebody who would *make* me leave. Roberto did that. I didn't think it would upset the whole world. . . ."

—INGRID BERGMAN; leaving husband Petter Lindstrom for Roberto Rossellini created a national scandal

"I want to tell you clearly that I will defend Ingrid in her
fear for you. It is unjust that you have made her
frightened.... I hope that you will understand that one cannot
condemn a big love and it is impossible to do anything against
it. I have begun my divorce, and now, Petter, please let
us be human, understand and have mutual respect."

> —ROBERTO ROSSELLINI, in a letter to Petter Lindstrom asking for
> his agreement to divorce Ingrid Bergman

2 percent of
daughters   } think their mothers have extra-
2 percent of sons } marital affairs.

26 percent of mothers have extramarital affairs.

"I know we talked about how many of your friends had divorced
parents. It is nothing unusual but it is rather sad. You have
to be for Papa both a daughter and 'wife,' and you'll have
all the time with him that I used to have. Take good care
of him. Your friends will naturally talk to you because as you
know with me it is out in the newspapers. There is nothing
to be ashamed of. Just say, yes, my parents are separated."

> —INGRID BERGMAN, in a letter to Pia explaining her divorce
> from Petter Lindstrom

"We deliberately built her up as the normal, healthy, nonneurotic
career woman devoid of scandal and with an idyllic
homelife. I guess that backfired later."

> —DAVID O. SELZNICK, on Ingrid Bergman

"Some people say Ingrid Bergman showed courage when she
left her first husband for her lover, Rossellini. But that
wasn't courage, that was lust."

> —JANET FLEISHHACKER, San Francisco civic leader

". . . My father was entertaining other relationships and it was no longer viable for my parents to live as a couple. It must have hurt my mother, but it was not strange to us, since it was all we knew. When we were 10 or 11, we began to realize that the other women had a place other than simple friendship. That was hurtful, because I was very protective and loved my mother very much. As a child, when you fear the answers, you don't ask a lot of questions."

> —ANGELICA HUSTON, on her parents—director John Huston and Ricki Soma. Soma was Huston's fourth wife.

7 percent of daughters
12 percent of sons
} think their fathers have extra-marital affairs.

50 percent of fathers have extramarital affairs.

"I'm a victim of Elizabeth Taylor's passion."

> —CARRIE FISHER, when asked if she wore Taylor's Passion perfume. She was 2 years old when her father, Eddie Fisher, left her mother, Debbie Reynolds, to marry "dear friend" Liz Taylor.

"My mama told me you don't do that. I was told I should fight him [Richard Burton], that if you blew on him he would fall over, but I'm not a fighter. So I left."

> —EDDIE FISHER, on Elizabeth Taylor's affair with Richard Burton

"If a woman and her adulterer are killed by her husband or fiancé, he shall pay no fine for the homicide, nor be sentenced to death."

> —SPANISH LAW, 1240

Stuck on You

In São Paulo, Brazil, a husband discovering his wife with another man, glued her hand to the lover's penis with acrylic cement. Despite successful surgery to separate the body parts, the man died several days later of toxic poisoning from the cement being absorbed into his bloodstream.

"If my wife cheated, I'd kill her. She's part of my property. I feel I *own* her, the way I own my car. And I don't lend my car."

—AL GOLDSTEIN, American publisher, 1973

"One of the things that made the strongest impression on me was seeing Onassis naked. He didn't seem to be a man, but a gorilla. He was very hairy. Maria looked at him and laughed."

—GIOVANNI BATTISTA MENEGHINI, Maria Callas's ex-husband, describing Aristotle Onassis during the Callas/Onassis affair aboard the *Christina* in 1959.

"The best way of revenging yourself on a man who has stolen your wife is to leave her to him."

—SACHA GUITRY

"One man's folly is another man's wife."

—HELEN ROWLAND, *Reflections of a Bachelor Girl*

Trying Times

Police in Doylestown, Pennsylvania, arrested Alfons Kessler, 47, for attempting to murder his girlfriend's husband. It was Kessler's fifth attempt at killing the man. He had been unsuccessful using a gun, a truck, a Molotov cocktail, and a crossbow, and this time was unsuccessful using a pipe bomb.

"Never approach a friend's girlfriend or wife with mischief as your goal. There are just too many women in the world to justify that sort of dishonorable behavior. Unless she's *really* attractive."

—BRUCE JAY FRIEDMAN

50 percent of divorced women ⎱ say their marriages
22 percent of divorced men ⎰ had interfered with their friendships.

"The hard thing is to be married with style. Being single is a breeze. Nowadays, you can have a head-on collision on Sunset Boulevard and end up going home with the girl you hit."

—GEORGE HAMILTON

"Do your own scientific study: Go to a shopping center on a Saturday. Stand outside a Kmart or a Wal-mart or a Sears or any of them. Look at the faces of the couples. Count the ones that look happy. Then count the ones who look miserable. You'll see: It's 98 percent gloom and 2 percent cheer. And that 2 percent are probably not married but are just sneaking around on the side."

—MIKE ROYKO

"The thing that hurts most marriages is that the husband or wife thinks there is someone else out there who's better. And they don't even know they've got it. People abandon a marriage for some small thing—as if there are nine other guys waiting to be your partner and who are going to love your children the way you do. . . ."

—SUSAN SAINT-JAMES

"It's not an affair. It's something that has been going on for a long time . . . it's a natural continuation of our friendship. . . .

Rosey and I didn't even kiss. We had been falling in love all those years, but we denied it to ourselves and everyone else. We never acted out our feelings because we didn't want to lose each other over a stupid thing we would later regret."

> —TOM ARNOLD, on his relationship with Roseanne Barr before her divorce from Bill Pentland

"Kathy has been faithful. Kathy knows I have not been. And she knows this because I told her. Every once in a while, I have stepped outside our relationship, but I have always come back and told her.... I have been loyal since we've been married. When you work in a candy store, your appetite for candy tends to diminish after a while."

> —BOB GUCCIONE, *Penthouse* magazine publisher, on marrying Kathy Keeton, an executive in Guccione's media company, after their 23-year engagement. This is his third marriage.

"I believe so much in marriage that I, myself, do not marry to avoid making a mistake. I do not discourage people from getting married. Those who get married after the age of thirty probably will have a happy marriage that includes physical faithfulness. If a man desires another woman, he is not totally happy with the one he has already."

> —HUGH HEFNER, 1966

"Angie told me about her marriage to Burt Bacharach. She knew about his affairs. She finally got all the evidence on him, detective agencies, the works. She was ready to throw him out and take him for all he was worth, even though she has as much money as he has. He walked into the house, and she was ready to pounce, but Burt said, 'I've gotta tell you something.' 'What?' 'I'm in love with Carole Bayer Sager. I'm leaving.' And all she could say was something like, 'You won't even give me the satisfaction of throwing you out!' "

> —LARRY KING, on Angie Dickinson, from *Tell It to the King*, 1988

> 25 percent of women ⎱ say infidelity by their spouses is
> 11 percent of men ⎰ a cause of divorce.

Hard Times

Charles Dickens sent an expensive gift to his mistress, Ellen Ternan, but by mistake gave the messenger his home address. Mrs. Dickens received the package and read the enclosed love letter. The marriage eventually disintegrated.

"When you marry your mistress, you automatically create a vacancy."

—Sir James Goldsmith

"If there were no husbands, who would look after our mistresses?"

—George Moore

"I have a wife and a mistress. From my wife I get love and understanding and sensitivity. From my mistress I get love and passion and sensuality. . . . It is a very Italian way. My wife understands that like a child I need to be always in the center of some interest. It demands great sacrifices of the woman. . . . I feel always a little guilty but not too much. Because . . . actors are children."

—Marcello Mastroianni

Call Girls

In the wake of adult phone lines like 1-900-HOT-BABE comes 1-900-MIS-TRES. It's exactly what it sounds like. For $5.95 a minute, tycoons, politicians, and other powerful folks can chat with a "mistress." The women on the other end of the line are trained "to make salacious comments about your golf-club collection, arrange assignations in small-town Marriots, beg you to leave your wife," and then threaten to expose the "affair."

"I don't want to be known as a man who steals another guy's wife. I want to be like my dad, home with my kids at night. It can be rough. Why is it people seem to expect a movie star to fail? They expect you to pay for your good luck—to see your marriage collapse. . . ."

—KEVIN COSTNER

"The lover thinks of possessing his mistress more often than her husband thinks of guarding his wife."

—STENDHAL

"The theater is like a faithful wife. The film is the great adventure—the costly, exacting mistress."

—INGMAR BERGMAN; after a stormy and scandalous affair with actress Liv Ullmann, he married for the sixth time

"One exists with one's husband—one lives with one's lover."

—BALZAC

"Husbands are chiefly good lovers when they are betraying their wives."

—MARILYN MONROE

"Nothing will make a model husband faster than infidelity."

—PETER DE VRIES, from *Madder Music,* 1977

"A lot of homes are ruined by inferior desecrators."

—FRANK LLOYD WRIGHT

"I felt incredibly guilty. I still feel that way. It was the hardest time I've ever had."

> —JILL EIKENBERRY, *L.A. Law* star, revealing that she ruined the first marriage of her current husband, Michael Tucker

21 percent of wives
26 percent of husbands } have been unfaithful

"Other offenses, however, were judged by her relatives together with her husband; among them was adultery, or where it was found she had drunk wine ... for Romulus permitted them to punish both these acts with death, as being the gravest offenses women could be guilty of.... And both these offenses continued for a long time to be punished by the Romans with merciless severity. The wisdom of this law concerning wives is attested by the length of time it was in force; for it is agreed that during the space of five hundred and twenty years no marriage was ever dissolved in Rome."

> —DIONYSIUS OF HALICARNASSUS, *The Roman Antiquities*, c. 25 B.C.

"I met him and liked what I saw. I wanted him. As anybody who's had a relationship with a married man knows, there's a great adrenaline rush with it. I didn't think about the consequences. I was a different person. I messed with people's lives. I feel bad if I hurt them, but I was just trying to figure it all out myself."

> —DEMI MOORE, on her affair with and marriage to guitarist Freddy Moore. They divorced four years later.

"You don't pick who you fall in love with. There are so few people to love. It's hard for one adult to even like the other. Almost impossible....

"I certainly had no intention of breaking up his relationship with his wife."

> —KATHARINE HEPBURN, on her 27-year affair with Spencer Tracy

Women's extramarital affairs last, on average, 21 months. Men's last 29 months.

Raising Cane

A 91-year-old woman sued her 79-year-old husband of 53 years for divorce in Queens, New York, accusing him of having an affair with a "younger woman," age 70. According to the lawsuit, her husband admitted to having been seeing the other woman for 40 years, and his wife decided to leave him when he became abusive and threatened to hit her with his cane. As the moving van pulled up to the house to take away her belongings, all her husband could say was, "Did you wash my clothes?"

"A woman who commits adultery with a man of a lower caste, the king shall cause to be devoured by dogs in a public place."
—GAUTAMA, *The Sacred Laws*, Hindu Scripture, c. A.D. 350

"I once knew a woman who did go out with a married man and I judged her too harshly. I felt it was wrong. It's a betrayal. To me, marriage is forever. I had no respect for any man who would ever think of cheating on his wife.... What I've learned is that nothing is black and white. Sometimes our biggest fears and hypocrisies come back to haunt us and teach us lessons...."
—MARLA MAPLES, 1990

Teachers' Petting

A New Hampshire schoolteacher admitted having an affair with a teenage student, but denied she coerced him to kill her newlywed husband, Gregory. Pamela Smart, 23, said she had sex with Wil-

liam Flynn three times, but insisted she never stopped loving her
husband and tried to end the affair with the student, who she said
threatened suicide and begged her to get a divorce. Asked why she
never told police of the affair, even after Flynn was arrested, Smart
said she did not believe he murdered her husband and was embarrassed by the relationship. "I had mixed feelings about it. . . . I
liked Bill, but I also loved Greg," Smart said.

"God knows it was not from debauchery for which I have never
had any inclination. If in my youth I had had a husband whom
I could have loved I should have remained faithful to him
all my life. It is my misfortune that my heart cannot rest
content, even for an hour, without love."
>   —CATHERINE THE GREAT; before and during her reign she had a series
>   of publicly admitted lovers and had several children out
>   of wedlock

"Your idea of fidelity is not having more than one man in bed
at the same time."
>   —DIRK BOGARDE, in *Darling,* screenplay by Frederic Raphael

"Talk about complicated! I was so overwhelmed that ever
since I've been trying to simplify my life. It was a *mess.*"
>   —JESSICA LANGE; in 1982 she was divorcing Paco Grande, living
>   with Mikhail Baryshnikov, and sleeping with Sam
>   Shepard

"The Regent Beverly-Wilshire Hotel is the best place for flings.
If you're caught in the lobby, you could claim you were going
to Buccellati jewelers, which has a branch there. Then
there's the Bel-Air Hotel. You walk over a little bridge to
enter, and it's very discreet. The Beverly Hills Hotel is a little
dangerous, unless you get a bungalow on the side street."
>   —JACKIE COLLINS, on the best places to have an affair in
>   Hollywood

"Adultery is a delightful way to spend the afternoon. It's sociable
and nonfattening."
>   —GAEL GREENE

"There are women whose infidelities are the only link they still have with their husbands."

—SACHA GUITRY

More than 75 percent of U.S. men surveyed on attitudes toward marriage said they were certain their wives would never cheat, but nearly 35 percent of the women questioned said they already had. The survey showed a similar discrepancy between wives' expectations and their husband's infidelity.

"I told my wife the truth. I told her I was seeing a psychiatrist. Then she told *me* the truth: that she was seeing a psychiatrist, two plumbers and a bartender."

—RODNEY DANGERFIELD

"Honesty has ruined more marriages than infidelity."

—CHARLES MCCABE, *San Francisco Chronicle* columnist

"Never tell. Not if you love your wife. . . . In fact, if your old lady walks in on you, deny it. Yeah. Just flat out and she'll believe it."

—LENNY BRUCE

"To Hillary Clinton—the modern 'no excuses' wife, who doesn't care how many ladies there are, as long as she's the first lady."

—NO EXCUSES JEANS AD FEATURING BILL AND HILLARY CLINTON

"I'm not sitting here like some little woman standing by my man like Tammy Wynette."

—HILLARY CLINTON, on *60 Minutes* discussing charges of her husband's infidelity

"I cannot have somebody whose mind shuts down if a good-lookin' woman shows up. . . . I want a person who's in a senior position busy serving the people, not chasing around every night, trying to toe-dance between his responsibilities to his family and his latest hot chick."

—H. ROSS PEROT

Donald and Ivana Trump

Trumped . . .

"We met at the Montreal Summer Olympic Games in August, 1976. I'd dated a lot of different women by then, but I'd never gotten seriously involved with any of them. Ivana wasn't someone you dated casually. Nine months later, in April, 1977, we were married."

—DONALD TRUMP, *Trump: The Art of the Deal*, 1987

And Dumped

"After a period of time—you know, you have the first year, the first few years—but after a period of time, doesn't this happen with everybody? And you would hope that it wouldn't, but probably in many cases it would. . . . I'm not the world's happiest person."

—DONALD TRUMP, on his split with Ivana, March 5, 1990

A Year of Trumpery

1990

February 12   Billionaire Donald Trump ends his 12-year marriage to Ivana Trump because "it just wasn't working out."

February 13   Ivana Trump wants more than the roughly $25 million agreed to in their prenuptial.

New and shocking insights into their breakup are revealed:
Among key disclosures—accounts of a Christmas holiday spat between Ivana and Donald's alleged mistress, *Maximum Overdrive* star Marla Maples, who is quoted as saying, "I love him and if you don't, why don't you let him go?" Ivana reportedly curses and calls her "Moolah," at which point Donald declares they are "just friends."

February 15	"Ivana doesn't want the money, she wants Donald. She totally loves me."—Donald Trump
February 16	It is the week that Nelson Mandela is freed, the two Germanys surge toward reunification, the Soviets agree to radical troop reductions in Europe, Bush travels to Colombia to form an "antidrug cartel," and Drexel Burnham files for bankruptcy. But the headlines read: BEST SEX I'VE EVER HAD, SAYS MARLA. The headline king of the hour, "The Donald" himself says, "The show is Trump and it is sold-out performances everywhere."
February 17	Donald considers a reconciliation for the sake of sons Donald, Jr., 12, Eric, 6, and daughter Ivancka, 8.
February 18	"[Marla] is a nice person who is merely a good friend."—Donald
February 20	The William Morris Agency announces that it is now booking Ivana "to speak at any of your upcoming events."

April 26	Donald and Ivana sign a pact that allows them to date without it becoming grounds for divorce. Sources say the pact was drawn up by Ivana, who wants to date but doesn't want to diminish any divorce settlement.
May 25	Marla begins her new job as spokeswoman for No Excuses jeans with Donald's blessings. "He's absolutely supportive. . . . He thinks it's a wonderful idea," Maples says. She signs a one-year contract for a reported $500,000.
June 29	Marla Maples's dad, Stan, files a $12 million libel suit against *The National Enquirer* for its recent journalistic endeavor, "MARLA'S ANGRY DAD WARNS: TRUMP MISTRESS CLOSE TO SUICIDE. HE THREATENS TO PUNCH OUT DONALD FOR DUMPING HER."
August 19	"I was humiliated by what people were allowed to believe—by the false perception of me. I wanted to scream out the truth, tell them I AM NOT A HOMEWRECKER, that people go through divorce, that life is a series of cycles, that people are allowed to be in love."—Marla Maples
September 9	*Spy* magazine reports that Donald and Marla are definitely intimate.
December 12	The Divorce of the Decade is granted. Donald is pronounced cruel and inhuman and Ivana leaves the courtroom in tears.
1991 February 14	The private eye Donald hired to spy on Ivana's private eye sues Trump for $5,394.90 in unpaid fees.

Spring Has Sprung

March 23	Donald and Ivana officially bring down the curtain and settle on a divorce deal. Although Ivana fails to change their prenuptial agreement, this is what she *does* get: $14 million in cash, a home in Connecticut, a penthouse apartment in New York City, use of the 118-room Trump mansion in Florida one month a year, $350,000 a year in alimony, and $300,000 annually to support their three children.
April 13	On Ivana's plastic surgery, Donald declares, "I can't stand to touch those plastic breasts."
June 27	Donald swaps Marla for Carla Bruni—an Italian model—and decides to pursue others.
June 29	After breaking up with Marla, Donald tells of his first verbal testing of the romantic waters: "Hi there, how about letting my personal physician give you an AIDS test? Can't be too careful. It's one of the worst times in the history of the world to be dating."

Summer Lovin'

July 2	Donald gives Marla a $250,000 flawless 7.5-carat diamond engagement ring from Harry Winston.
July 3	Donald announces on live television his engagement to Marla: "She's something special. It's worked out great."
July 5	Donald explains why he dumped Marla only to propose to her a week later: "I spent one week being single, and single life isn't what it used to be. I didn't like being free as much as I thought I would. I love her, she's spectacular."

July 15 Marla Maples says she won't sign a prenuptial agreement with Donald. "I don't think we're doing it that way. . . . That makes things so shallow. . . . This relationship is going to be based on trust."

The Fall Arrives

September 14 Donald becomes infatuated with Miss America—Carolyn Sapp. Marla reports that at one point, Donald approached the contestants and announced, "I want to see the bodies that won the swimsuit contest!" Sapp stepped forward and introduced herself. Marla described her as "very brazen." From that point on, Maples says, Donald remained fixated and made constant references to Sapp's anatomy. "I don't think it's very respectful," says Marla. "I deserve better than that."

September 23 They were on. Then they were off. Then they were on again. And now Donald says he's broken up with Marla—this time for good.

1992
April 18 A New York court backs Donald and places a gag order on Ivana. Her book, *For Love Alone,* is apparently a thinly veiled account of their life together. The state appeals court restores the terms of their divorce, barring Ivana from publicly talking about their marriage. Donald's attorney, Jay Goldberg, says he might sue Ivana to recover "all monies received by her misusing confidential information. . . . Every time she opens up her mouth about this book, she's working for Donald."

April 26

Donald thinks about not paying his next alimony payment of $350,000, due in August. His attorney says that Ivana, the novelist, "totally violated" their divorce agreement with loose talk and writings and cited her remark to Barbara Walters on national TV that she had gotten the Deal Artist's "last 10 million." Donald says, "I don't have to pay. . . . But I haven't given it much thought. I have always paid child support—$300,000—and I will continue to pay [that]."

June 30

Donald's lawyer asks a judge to cancel alimony obligations to Ivana because she is living with another man. Ivana is living and traveling with Riccardo Mazzucchelli, who cooks for her and keeps his clothes and vitamin pills at her house, attorney Jay Goldberg tells Justice Phyllis Gangel-Jacob. Ivana's attorney denies she is living with Mazzucchelli. Included in court papers is an affidavit by Minna Laputina, who resigned May 13 after working as Mrs. Trump's social secretary for eight months. Laputina said her boss often expressed her love for, and desire to marry, Mazzucchelli. Goldberg says Mrs. Trump told Laputina she intended to marry Mazzucchelli but wanted to wait "at least another year so that [Donald] can pay me more money." Said Donald: "If she cohabits, she doesn't get paid. She's living the jet-set life; let him pay for it. I've given her $25 million. That's enough, don't you think?"

Trumped . . .

"I'd felt that I needed space and freedom after the divorce, so I took the opportunity to go out with other women, but I kept coming back to Marla. I realized, why go looking for something when you already have exactly what you want?"

—DONALD TRUMP

And Dumped—Again

"I want to remain good friends with her. But it's time to step aside and look in other directions."

—DONALD TRUMP, on Marla

Winter, Spring, Summer or Fall?

1992
July 11   Okay, maybe it's not completely over. Donald and Marla may actually wed during the winter. Marla says she and Donald will be married during the first break from her Broadway debut in *The Will Rogers Follies*. That break will probably be in the wintertime. Marla says, "I've always wanted a winter wedding."

Falling on Your A$$ets

"I never took money from anybody in my divorces. I'm psychopathically independent."

> —LINA BASQUETTE, actress in *The Godless Girl,* Cecil B. De Mille's last silent film. Sam Warner made her a wife at 18, a mother at 19, and a widow at 20. She then remarried and divorced.

Keeping Up with the Khashoggis . . . Some Celebrated Divorce Settlements:

$800 million plus property: Soraya Khashoggi, from Saudi Arabian financier Adnan Khashoggi

$112 million: Frances Lear, from TV mogul Norman Lear

$100 million: Amy Irving, from Steven Spielberg

$81 million: Sheika Dena al-Fassi, from Saudi Arabian Sheik Mohammad al-Fassi. (She originally sought $3 billion.)

$41 million: Jeannie Cooke, from tycoon Jack Kent Cooke

$16 million: Julianne Phillips, from Bruce Springsteen
$13 million: Noelene Hogan, from actor Paul Hogan
$6 million: Brigitte Nielsen, from Sylvester Stallone
$4 million: Joan Kennedy, from Senator Edward Kennedy

"Never mind my husband, where's my Lamborghini?
  —SORAYA KHASHOGGI, ex-wife of Adnan Khashoggi, on being told
    that her (now-ex) husband, Robert Rupley, was seen living
    it up in London with a blonde

Sheik Deal

Belgian-born Sheika Dena al-Fassi, 23, filed the highest ever alimony claim of $3 billion against her former husband, Sheik
Mohammad al-Fassi, 28, of the Saudi Arabia royal family, in Los
Angeles, California, in 1982. Explaining the size of the settlement
claim, lawyer Marvin Mitchelson alluded to the sheik's wealth,
which included 14 homes in Florida alone and numerous private
aircraft. When in 1983 she was awarded $81 million, she declared
herself "very, very happy" if she was able to collect.

"I think he loved me. As much as a man like that could love. . . .
He used to say, 'Suzanne, if I didn't have all this money, you
wouldn't love me.' "
  —SUZANNE MARTIN COOKE, second ex-wife of Jack Kent Cooke.
    His first divorce made the *Guinness Book of World Records*
    when he gave his wife of 42 years, $41 million.
    The Washington Redskins, the Chrysler Building, and
    the *L.A. Daily News* are a few of Cooke's
    many financial assets.

"There's no way Frankie [Sylvester's father] would pay alimony
like Sylvester does to these nobodies. Sasha [Stallone's first
wife] was a girl who got a lift from New York to Los
Angeles so that she could watch his dogs. A year later, he
makes *Rocky* and she goes for $20 million in alimony. And

then, Brigitte Nielsen, this beast, comes along right behind her. I could see if the girls had contributed something. You know, if they'd gotten married and struggled side by side. It doesn't seem fair."

—JACQUELINE STALLONE, on her son's divorces

"I don't think I'll ever marry again. I've been scorched too much. I'm very difficult to live with. I make a much better boyfriend than I do a husband."

—SYLVESTER STALLONE, twice divorced; his first divorce cost him
$20 million and his second, to Brigitte Nielsen,
ended after three years with a $6 million settlement

"Would I consider remarriage? If I found a man who had $15 million, would sign over half of it to me before marriage, and guarantee he'd be dead within a year."

—BETTE DAVIS

Ain't Life Grands

A woman serving 10 years for her husband's death has inherited $25,000 of his money. Anne Gates was charged with first-degree murder in 1987 after her husband, Raymond, was beaten to death with a fireplace poker in Arabi, just outside New Orleans. Anne Gates pleaded no contest to manslaughter in 1989. Anyone convicted of murder can be removed from the victim's will in Louisiana. However, Gates's lawyers said that didn't apply to her because a no-contest plea does not admit guilt.

"We both had one thing in common. We both wanted his money. . . ."

—ZSA ZSA GABOR, on ex-husband Conrad Hilton

"She knew more days on which gifts could be given than appear on any holiday calendar."

—CONRAD HILTON, on Zsa Zsa Gabor

"Each [of my wives] was jealous and resentful of my preoccupation with business. Yet none showed any visible aversion to sharing the proceeds."

—J. PAUL GETTY

"The trouble is that nothing can be a gift when the man holds legal and financial power over you. How can one love one's keeper? That's the question. You don't have a lover. You have a keeper. One of the things my ex-husband said when we split was, 'The next time I get married, all the bankbooks will be in my name.' "

—ERICA JONG

"I believe in marriage . . . but there ain't going to be no equality. If you want to be equal with me, you can get your own Rolls-Royce, your own house, and your own million dollars."

—MUHAMMAD ALI, 1979, divorced three times

Satan Sale

Because he owes money to his common-law wife, Church of Satan founder Anton La Vey has been ordered by a judge to sell his San Francisco home, known as the "Black House," and all his belongings. Sale items include a shrunken head, a reproduction of Tutankhamen's sarcophagus, an antique Egyptian skull, a stuffed wolf, two fake machine guns, an assortment of automatic pistols, two crossbows, and a classic "Rockola" jukebox.

"I don't think I'll get married again. I'll just find a woman I don't like and give her a house."

—LEWIS GRIZZARD, divorced three times

Halfway House

Eugene Schneider of Carteret, New Jersey, cut his $80,000 home in half with a chain saw in July 1976 after his wife sued him for divorce, thus fulfilling in his eyes the equal division of property required by New Jersey law.

Encouraged by this case, Virgil M. Everhart of Central City, Kentucky, 57, chopped and sawed away at his house with TV cameras turned on, on January 20, 1983. He was stopped by a judge who criticized his "cute trick" and made an alimony award to his wife instead.

"Oliver and Barbara Rose were both civilized grown-ups. They could certainly handle a divorce. Naturally, Oliver was a bit put out when Barbara told him out of the blue that she wanted one. And of course Barbara had a few little resentments that had simmered under the surface for a number of years. But that wouldn't get in the way as they squared off to decide how to split everything they had in two. What happened then would make Attila the Hun take notes. . . ."
—THE WAR OF THE ROSES, novel by Warren Adler

"When I got married all the property was put in two names. My wife's. And her mother's."
—RODNEY DANGERFIELD

"Trust your husband, adore your husband, and get as much as you can in your own name."
—JOAN RIVERS

Socked Away

Palm Beach millionaire, James Sullivan, accused his wife Suki Sullivan of secretly hoarding clothes, jewelry, perfume, and more than 400 packages of panty hose before filing for her divorce.

"The difference between divorce and legal separation is that
a legal separation gives a husband time to hide his money."

—JOHNNY CARSON

"Prior to the Olympics it was 'our' money; afterward it
became 'his' money."

—CHRYSTIE JENNER, on ex-husband Bruce Jenner

Home Run

A Montana court ruled that Michael Keedy and his ex-wife must
get equal value from Keedy's baseball card collection because it
was a "marital asset." The court said the wife helped safeguard and
maintain the collection and that the family budget suffered so
Keedy could accumulate the 100,000 cards, which are worth as
much as $200,000. Keedy maintained that the cards bought before
the marriage should be his.

"Many men hoard for the future husbands of their wives."

—SOLOMON IBN GABIROL, medieval Jewish philosopher,
Pearls of Wisdom

"I bequeath all my property to my wife on the condition
that she remarry immediately. Then there will be at least one
man to regret my death."

—HEINE

Tackling It Out

A fight between a Washington, D.C., couple over who would get
the Redskins' season tickets resulted in a legal battle that cost each
$50,000 in lawyers fees.

"Marriage, a market which has nothing free but the entrance."

—MONTAIGNE

"In love, you pay as you leave."

—MARK TWAIN

Don't Leave Home Without It

Dade County, Florida, courts have decided to accept MasterCard and Visa for such services as adoptions, marriages, wills, lawsuits, and—divorces. "It's our way of saying, 'Welcome to the 21st Century,' " said Marshall Ader, clerk of the circuit and county courts. Ader envisions everyone using it—from legal firms to divorced dads "temporarily embarrassed" by a lack of cash to pay child support.

"Many unusual things do occur at weddings. . . . Like the wedding where the father of the groom—divorced and behind in alimony— joined his son at the altar and was promptly served a subpoena by his ex-wife."

—JUDITH VIORST

"We got married in Las Vegas. A Vegas wedding strips the act of getting married of all the extraneous stuff; it's all business. They try to inject a little romance into it, but when you're getting married at four in the morning and you see them slip the organ music cassette into the tape player, some of the majesty is removed. I still have the Visa receipt: 'Wedding: $45.' Aside from giving children a real last name, I've yet to find a use for marriage. Aside from fueling the alimony industry."

—HARRY SHEARER, actor/writer, host of *Le Show* on
National Public Radio

"You never saw any husband writing an alimony check in Norman Rockwell's America."

—GEORGE MENDOZA, *The New York Times,* 1985

" 'Give 'em anything they want, but never marry 'em' "
has always been my credo. As charter member of the Bachelor's
Club, I had been preaching this gospel since the day I issued
my first alimony check."

—JOEY ADAMS, *Cindy and I*

"She cried—and the judge wiped her tears with my checkbook."

—TOMMY MANVILLE, divorced 11 times

"Judges, as a class, display, in the matter of arranging
alimony, that reckless generosity which is found only in
men who are giving away someone else's cash."

—P. G. WODEHOUSE

"The wages of sin is alimony."

—CAROLYN WELLS, American writer and humorist

"Alimony—the ransom that the happy pay to the devil."

—H. L. MENCKEN, "Sententiae," *A Book of Burlesques*

"Alimony is a system by which one pays for the mistake
of two."

—JOHN GARLAND POLLARD

"Alimony—the curse of the writing classes."

—NORMAN MAILER

"Alimony—billing minus cooing."

—MARY DORSEY

"Alimony—disinterest, compounded annually."

—WALTER MCDONALD

"Alimony: bounty after the mutiny."

—MAX KAUFFMANN

"If income tax is the price we have to pay to keep the government
on its feet, alimony is the price we have to pay for sweeping
a woman off hers."

—GROUCHO MARX, divorced from Ruth Johnson in 1942
after a 22-year marriage

Over-Taxed

Michael Friend won his appeal of the IRS's denial of several 1980 deductions he had claimed in a joint return with his then-wife (involving her medical expenses and job-related education). Friend celebrated the news in a Kentucky prison. He will now enjoy a lower tax bill because of the deductions taken by the woman he was convicted of murdering the following year.

"Henry VIII . . . didn't get divorced, he just had [his wives'] heads chopped off when he got tired of them. That's a good way to get rid of a woman—no alimony."

—TED TURNER

"Old wives don't die if they're getting alimony."

—DAVID BROWN

About 6 percent of women still collect alimony.

"A lot of women who are getting alimony don't earn it."

—DON HEROLD

"Even hooligans marry, though they know that marriage is but for a little while. It is alimony that is forever."

—QUENTIN CRISP

"You never realize how short a month is until you pay alimony."

—JOHN BARRYMORE

"A fool and his money are soon parted, but at least the money doesn't ask for alimony."

—MARK O'DONNELL, newspaper columnist

"Alimony is like buying oats for a dead horse."

—ARTHUR "BUGS" BAER, sportswriter

"The alimonized wife bringing up the children without father
is no more free than she ever was."

　　　　　　　　　　　—GERMAINE GREER, *The Female Eunuch*

In the year following a divorce the woman's standard of
living falls by 73 percent, the man's standard of living
rises by 42 percent.

"If I hadn't married John, I probably would have been a simple
housewife growing old."

　　　　—JODY WOLCOTT CARSON; she obtained a Mexican divorce in
　　　　　　1963 and was granted $15,000 a year in alimony,
　　　　　　$7,500 in child support, and 15 percent of Carson's gross
　　　　　　earnings over $100,000

Today, nationally, five years after divorce, a woman's income is 30 percent of what it was during the marriage.
A man's income is 14 percent more.

"No one is going to take Women's Liberation seriously until
women recognize that they will not be thought of as equals
in the secret privacy of men's most private parts until they
eschew alimony."

　　　　　　　　　　　　　　　—NORMAN MAILER

"Anyone dealing with him should realize that the man is an
alimony slave."

　　　　　　　　　　—GERMAINE GREER, on Norman Mailer

"Will you still love me when I don't have any money?"
　　—DONALD TRUMP, to Ivana during a June 1990 reconciliation attempt

"Yes, I already did love you when you didn't have any
money, remember?"

　　　　　　　—IVANA TRUMP, replying to The Donald, June 1990

"A judge in New York had ruled that panhandlers do not have the right to beg for money according to the Constitution. Guess that means Donald Trump is going to have to get those alimony payments another way."

—JAY LENO

"Marla Maples assures us she's marrying Donald Trump for love, not for money. Of course. Everyone knows you marry for love. You divorce for money."

—JAY LENO

"Get a huge engagement ring. It is considered separate property and cannot be pledged as collateral against any future husband's debt. . . . As a rich man's wife, you'll be making new friends whom you can later betray for big bucks. Keep track of all the juicy stuff. Think book deal, miniseries. You can never underestimate America's fascination with crass wealth."

—*NEW YORK WOMAN* MAGAZINE, providing Marla Maples with pre- and post-wedding advice, April 1991

"I have never hated a man enough to give his diamonds back."

—ZSA ZSA GABOR

The Bear Facts

After one Chicago woman absconded with the divorcing couple's beanbag chairs, the man retaliated by taking the teddy bear she slept with. She went to court to regain custody.

"No longer is the female destined for the home and the rearing of the family and only the male for the marketplace and the world of ideas."

—WILLIAM J. BRENNAN, Associate Justice, U.S. Supreme Court, majority opinion in 6-3 ruling that laws barring alimony for men are unconstitutional, 1979

Galimony

(Women paying men alimony)
 Roseanne Barr Arnold
 Kim Basinger
 Seema Silberstein Boesky
 Joan Collins (request denied)
 Phyllis Diller
 Jane Fonda
 Goldie Hawn
 Jessica Lange
 Linda Lavin (request denied)
 Joan Lunden
 Mary McFadden
 Jane Seymour
 Lana Turner (request denied)

"I think this decision is a deplorable and shameful statement
on how working women are treated today when we've supported
our families and been totally responsible for our children.
Why the courts don't tell a husband who has been living
off his wife to go out and get a job is beyond my comprehension."
>   —JOAN LUNDEN, responding to a court petition from her future
>   ex-husband, TV producer Michael Krauss, who is
>   seeking $18,000 a month in temporary support from
>   the *Good Morning America* host.

"Here you have a man working side by side with his wife,
pushing her career, and suddenly she says, 'You should get
a job.' That's not so easy after 14 years."
>   —MICHAEL KRAUSS'S LAWYER, on seeking alimony from Joan Lunden

"[I gave him] a big chunk of money. There was no reason
I had to. There was a moment where it made me really
angry. Then I started thinking back and thought, I had the
money, he didn't. This is how we always lived our lives. He
would've given it to me if he had it."
>   —JESSICA LANGE, on paying ex-husband, Paco Grande, alimony

"I'm virtually wiped out."

—IVAN BOESKY; Boesky, 55, was sued for divorce by his wife of
30 years, Seema Silberstein Boesky, the daughter of a real-estate
magnate. Boesky retaliated in April 1992 by suing Seema for
$1 million a year in temporary alimony. Ivan Boesky was a
billionaire until he was brought down by fines and prison time
in Wall Street's junk bond scandal. The Boeskys have a penthouse
in Manhattan and a mansion in Westchester, both in Seema's
name. In 1991, Mrs. Boesky sought possession of Mr. Boesky's
Honolulu condominium when, she said, he failed to pay interest
on $2.3 million in loans from her. Trying to keep their affairs private,
the Boeskys, who have four grown children, have traded shots
in State Supreme Court in Manhattan as *Anonymous I* v.
Anonymous II.

"JOAN, YOU HAVE OUR $2.5 MILLION 13,000-SQ. FT. HOME WHICH
WE BOUGHT FOR CASH DURING OUR MARRIAGE. I AM NOW
HOMELESS. HELP!

　　　—PETER HOLM, picketing Joan Collins during their divorce trial

"Throughout our marriage I have dressed stylishly. I have spent
large sums updating my wardrobe to enhance my wife's
public image. I spent approximately $20,000 per month on
clothing and accessories. . . . In fact, during our marriage we
withdrew over $600,000 in cash for these kinds of
expenditures. . . . Because I am presently unemployed, and
all savings during the marriage were invested in our Cabrillo
home, my cash flow is, at present, zero. Therefore, I am requesting
$80,000 per month in order that I can maintain my standard
of living which I have enjoyed previous to and during our
marriage. . . ."

　　　—PETER HOLM, Request for Spousal Support, filed in California
　　　　Superior Court in 1987. Joan Collins filed for divorce from
　　　　Holm after 13 months of marriage.

Going for Broker

Steve Lane, chief executive officer of Emerson Radio Corporation, suffered $12 million in losses on October 1987's Black Monday, and sued Drexel Burnham Lambert for incompetence. Lane's Drexel broker was his wife, Trina.

33 percent of women ⎱ say money problems are a
29 percent of men   ⎰ cause of divorce.

Heeeere's Johnny, Jody, Joanne, and Joanna . . .

"I resolve that if I ever again get hit in the face with rice, it will be because I insulted a Chinese person."

—JOHNNY CARSON

Carson Productions

Wife number one was Jody Wolcott Carson. They were married in Nebraska and had three sons together. Their divorce was the simplest of them all. They separated in 1959 and obtained a quick Mexican divorce.

"You may think that my giving advice on marriage is like the captain of the *Titanic* giving lessons on navigation."

—JOHNNY CARSON

Carson Reductions

Wife number two was Joanne Copeland, an airline stewardess he met in New York City in 1963. Seven years later, Joanne left

Johnny. She felt that he spent too much time working on *The To-night Show*—leaving little time to spend with her. After a protracted divorce, Joanne ended up with nearly half a million dollars in cash and art and $100,000 a year in alimony for life.

"My producer, Freddy de Cordova, really gave me something I needed for Christmas. He gave me a gift certificate to the legal offices of Jacoby & Myers."

—JOHNNY CARSON

Wife number three was Joanna Holland, a 33-year-old former model that Johnny, 46, married on September 30, 1972. On March 8, 1983, Joanna filed for a divorce and the proceedings continued over the next two years. It ended in one of the largest settlements received by a wife for her husband's income and assets.

"I went to see my butcher the other day, Murray Giblets. I said, 'How do you pick a good turkey?' And he says, 'You ought to know. You're a three-time loser.' "

—JOHNNY CARSON

Carson Deductions

(Joanna's take)
   Mansion at 400 St. Cloud Road in Bel Air
   Hotel Pierre condominium in New York City
   Apartments at 201 East 62nd Street and 910 Fifth Avenue in
      New York
   1976 Rolls-Royce, 1976 Mercedes-Benz
   All the jewelry, clothing, and furs purchased during the marriage
   310 shares in Carson Broadcasting Corporation Stock
   One-half of all the stock in the Albuquerque Broadcasting Cor-
      poration
   $216,000 in cash from their tax fund
   Two Wells Fargo bank accounts
   RCA debentures
   Signal Corporation Stock
   One-half of several of Johnny's companies

$338,000 in accounts receivable

75 solid gold Krugerrands

$337,500 from the salary Johnny earned doing the annual *Tonight Show* anniversary shows.

A percentage of Johnny's AFTRA and Screen Actor's Guild pensions.

50 percent of all the money NBC will pay Johnny in the future for airing reruns of *Tonight Show*s that he starred in during their marriage.

$35,000 a month in alimony for five years—on the first of each month from September 1, 1985, to December 1, 1990. It was also ruled that if Johnny died anytime before December 1990, alimony payments would still have to be made on time, each month, from his estate.

Joanna also asked Johnny for $270.38 in "pet care." There was only one problem. Prior to their separation, she didn't own a pet. Johnny joked, "I heard from my cat's lawyer. My cat wants $12,000 a month for Tender Vittles."

Wife number four is Alex Maas. She became Johnny's June bride in 1987, when she was 35 and he was 61.

Carson Precautions

Johnny asked Alex to sign a prenuptial agreement limiting her take at less than 50 percent of his net worth in the event they ever divorced.

"An old lady stopped me on the street. She says, 'Johnny, I want a divorce from you.' And I say, 'But we're not married.' She says, 'Yeah, but I want to skip right to the goodies.' "

—JOHNNY CARSON

Pillow Talk

"Everybody makes me out to be some kind of macho pig, humping women in the gutter. I do, but I put a pillow under 'em first."

—JAMES CAAN, divorced twice

"Woman is a temple built upon a sewer."

—BOETHIUS, *The Consolation of Philosophy*, c. A.D. 500

Prince of Wales: "I've spent enough on you to buy a battleship."
Lillie Langtry: "And you've spent enough *in* me to float one."
(The Prince of Wales—Edward VII—was married to Alexandra when he and actress Lillie Langtry had an affair.)

18 percent of married couples together for 10 years or more have sex at least 3 times a week.

"What if I look great and what if men are being attracted to me? I'm tired of apologizing.... [Waiting for Jim is] too hard on the physical body."

—TAMMY FAYE BAKKER; seeking a divorce from
televangelist Jim Bakker who is serving 18
years for telephone and mail fraud

Members Only

In October 1991, a village council in Meru, Kenya, found a man guilty of having sex with his mother-in-law and two sisters-in-law and fined him one bull, one goat, and about $30 in cash. One of the village judges suggested castrating the man, according to the *Daily Nation* newspaper, but was overruled because the man's wife said she still needed the services of a "complete man."

Tuesday Weld: Harvey, I think it's time we communicated on . . . where this marriage is going.
Martin Mull: Goodbye, hard-on.
— *SERIAL*, screenplay by Rich Eustis and Michael Elias, 1980

5 percent of married women ⎱ sometimes argue with
9 percent of married men ⎰ their spouses over sex.

David Selby: I never drank to do my job at the lab; I only drank to perform my job as a husband!
Candice Bergen: Then you better bring a bottle to bed next time.
— *RICH AND FAMOUS*, screenplay by Gerald Ayres, 1981

"Nothing was happening in my marriage. I nicknamed our water bed Lake Placid."
— PHYLLIS DILLER, divorced twice

Down and Out

A 64-year-old woman sued her 71-year-old husband in Boulder, Colorado, because he had not been able to consummate the marriage in the one month since the wedding, after leading her to believe during courtship that he was capable. She claimed "severe mental anguish, personal humiliation . . . and financial losses" and sued for $50,000.

"During sex my wife wants to talk to me. The other night she called me from a hotel."

—RODNEY DANGERFIELD

"If you're contemplating marriage again, Barbara, dear, just remember to rotate your hips. It makes things more pleasant for the man."

—MARJORIE HUTTON, to her niece, 1934

| 59 percent of wives | } say their spouses are |
| 48 percent of husbands | skilled lovers. |

"Never ask your wife if she still hears from her old pimp."

—JOHNNY CARSON, divorced three times

"The difference between a wife and a prostitute is that the wife has a contract and a streetwalker free-lances."

—KATE MILLETT

"The highest peaks of sexual excitement in my life have always been in monogamy. . . . I grew up thinking I would marry the first woman I had sex with and would stay married to her for the rest of my life."

—WARREN BEATTY

"I've only slept with the men I've been married to. How many women can make that claim?"

—ELIZABETH TAYLOR, married eight times

"I know nothing about sex, because I was always married."

—ZSA ZSA GABOR

> **26 percent of women** } say they enjoy sex more than
> **47 percent of men** } money.

"Thank God, I am a virgin again."
>   —LYDIA LOPOKOVA, Russian ballet dancer and wife of economist
>   John Maynard Keynes, when their divorce became final

"When Woodrow proposed to me I was so surprised I nearly
fell out of bed."
>   —MRS. WOODROW WILSON, second wife of President Woodrow Wilson

"She never associated the idea of sex with sin. In this she
was a woman free from any guilt complex."
>   —ROGER VADIM, on Jane Fonda

> **32 percent of women** } say sexual problems are a
> **30 percent of men** } cause of divorce.

Thai Butterfly

An Italian businessman has asked a court to annul his eight-month
marriage to a Thai after learning his wife had a sex-change operation and was not a "genuine female."

"Hah! I always knew Frank would end up in bed with a boy."
>   —AVA GARDNER, on ex-husband Frank Sinatra's marriage to Mia
>   Farrow

Piano Man?

In 1989, jazz musician Billy Tipton died of a bleeding ulcer, leaving an ex-wife and three adopted sons. While the funeral director was preparing the body for burial, he discovered the 74-year-old saxophonist-pianist was really a woman. "He'll always be Dad," said one of Tipton's boys.

Return to Gender

Baltimore Judge Hilary Caplan voided the marriage of Liberian Prince M. K. Ofosu-Appiah, 28, to Delores Buchanan, on the grounds that Buchanan was a man. The prince, who claimed that he never saw Buchanan nude and never consummated the marriage, discovered that Delores was a man when he saw that her birth certificate had "male" in the section identifying sex.

"Sexually polarizing behavior and expectations is the road to disillusionment, disharmony, and divorce."

—Rita Mae Brown

Just Wild About Harriet

A 17-year-old Memphis woman was married for four months before discovering that her husband was a 19-year-old woman. According to a clergyman involved in the case, the woman said that her husband never let her see "him" naked because he was supposedly deformed by a football injury. The bride reportedly became suspicious when some of her husband's friends referred to him as "Harriet."

"If divorce has increased one thousand percent, don't blame

the woman's movement. Blame our obsolete sex roles on which
our marriages are based."

—BETTY FRIEDAN, 1974

"The chief cause of unhappiness in married life is that people
think that marriage is sex attraction, which takes the form of
promises and hopes and happiness—a view supported by
public opinion and by literature. But marriage cannot cause
happiness. Instead, it is always torture, which man has to pay
for satisfying his sex urge."

—LEO TOLSTOY; in 1862, he married Sophie Behrs, a marriage
that was to become, for him, bitterly unhappy

"The kind of things that they've been studying are going to
be waning in their own life. We all lose our facility with sexuality,
but it's going to be particularly upsetting when you've
devoted your whole life to studying it."

—FRANK COX, professor of psychology at Santa Barbara City College,
on the Masters and Johnson divorce. Associates of
William Masters, 76, say that he is obsessed with his work,
while Johnson, 67, yearns to travel. Others say they're both
strong-willed and clash over important ideas.

45 percent of married couples
61 percent of cohabitating couples
} who have been together up to two years have sex at least three times a week.

Advice Column

"The lady with all the answers does not know the answer to this one. . . . [This column] is a memorial to one of the world's best marriages that didn't make it to the finish line."
> —ANN LANDERS, in a column written when her 36-year marriage to Jules Lederer ended

"I love marriage. It's a wonderful idea. But it takes singular people committed to compromise, to support and care for each other. And life doesn't always allow for that. There's a way to do it well, sure. But only exceptional people can make it work."
> —MEREDITH BAXTER-BIRNEY, divorced twice

"What counts in making a happy marriage is not so much how compatible you are, but how you deal with incompatibility."
> —GEORGE LEVINGER

"I think wedding vows are peculiar—you promise to obey, promise this and that. That is so hypocritical. That's not how life is. In order to keep someone, you have to be willing to let go of them. A healthy relationship revolves around freedom."
> —LEE GRANT, divorced once and married to Joseph Feury since 1965

"I think that freedom and ability to close a chapter in our lives that isn't working—like getting a divorce—is really important. To pack up and move away. And do something else. I've done it, my parents have done it before me. I'm not saying that because *we* have the option it's good for everybody. It's something I struggle with. The way to check commitment is to understand it. I think I just may be able to do it now."

> —TOM HANKS, divorced in 1987 from Samantha Lewes and
> remarried to Rita Wilson in 1988

"Believing in true love, saving yourself for that true love, and having one husband for all your life just seems to me how things should be."

> —NANCY REAGAN

"Think twice before marrying a professional agitator."

> —ELDRIDGE CLEAVER, on his wife, Kathleen

53 percent of married people say that when couples argue over clothing expenses, the wife usually wins; 20 percent say the husband usually wins.

"The husband who wants a happy marriage should learn to keep his mouth shut and his checkbook open."

> —GROUCHO MARX

"When you're a married man, Samivel, you'll understand a good many things as you don't understand now; but vether it's worthwhile goin' through so much to learn so little, as the charity boy said ven he got to the end of the alphabet, is a matter o' taste."

> —CHARLES DICKENS, *Pickwick Papers*

Feminine Mystique

In Singapore, a woman was granted a divorce on the grounds that both she and her "husband" are female, a discovery she made on her wedding night. Lim Ying told the High Court she discovered that her husband, Eric Hiok Kian Ming, a forklift driver, was a woman who had a sex-change operation in 1987.

"Before you marry make sure you know whom you are going to divorce."

—YIDDISH PROVERB

"Say goodbye to your best friend at the wedding reception
. . . unless of course your best friend is of the opposite sex,
in which case you've married the wrong person."

—ANDREW WARD, *Atlantic Monthly*

"I guess walking slow getting married is because it gives
you time to maybe change your mind."

—VIRGINIA CARY HUDSON, American essayist

To Know-a-Veil

The *Times* of India reported that two Hindu brides, their vision obscured by long veils, married each other's grooms at Patan village ceremonies that were rushed because both had been mistakenly scheduled for the same time. Village elders said the marriages are final and cannot be revoked.

"Shutting one's eyes is an art, my dear. I suppose there's no use trying to make you see that—but that's the only way one *can* stay married."

—ZOË AKINS, American writer, *Daddy's Gone A-Hunting*

In the Eyes of the Beholder

In 1987, a 61-year-old retired Army sergeant shot a woman he mistook for his estranged wife outside a church in Rochester, New York. "I'm sorry about the other woman," he told police. "I meant to kill my wife, but I forgot my glasses."

"My old man used to say, 'If love is blind, marriage is like having a stroke.' "

> —GAVIN D'AMATO, divorce lawyer played by Danny DeVito in *The War of the Roses*

The Man Who Mistook His Wife for a Woodchuck

A Westchester, New York, man shot and killed his wife while hunting, telling police that he had mistaken her for a woodchuck.

"If a lady has been so unfortunate as to have married a man not a gentleman, to draw attention to his behavior would put herself on his level."

> —EMILY POST, on divorce, 1922

"Keep some mystery in your marriage—don't let your husband see you running around in torn panties and hair curlers. Make yourself beautiful in a private place. Don't live like brother and sister. Do all you can to keep the romance alive."

> —JACKIE COLLINS, on how to make a marriage last

"A relationship I think is . . . is like a shark. You know it has to constantly move forward or it dies."

> —WOODY ALLEN, from *Annie Hall*

"Whenever you want to marry someone, go have lunch with his ex-wife."

> SHELLEY WINTERS

"After years of advising other people on their personal
problems I was stunned by my own divorce. I only wish I
had someone to write for help."

—ANN LANDERS, divorced after a 36-year marriage

Supercouple of the Century

After mulling it over for a half-century, America's greatest superhero
has finally popped The Big Question. It's the engagement of Lois
Lane and Clark Kent (a.k.a. Superman). A 50-year courtship has
taken a dangerous turn. A guy who can leap tall buildings in a single
bound took a lot longer to settle down. So what are the chances for
a man who is faster than a speeding bullet and a career woman of the
1990s who can win a Pulitzer Prize but can't figure out where her
Clark goes when the world calls him on his beeper?

Leading experts offer their opinions:

"I think, darling, that by now they should know each other's
shortcomings. But I know a woman who dated a man for four
or five years before she married him. It was the end of
their love affair."

—ZSA ZSA GABOR

"It may be the longest foreplay I've ever heard of."

—DR. JOYCE BROTHERS

"A prenuptial agreement is very unromantic and it would
probably provide for a lot less than the law would allow her.
Plus [Clark Kent's income] is the salary of a reporter. There's
no need for a prenup, there's no money."

—MARVIN MITCHELSON, palimony lawyer

"I don't speculate on a couple's problems."

—DR. RUTH WESTHEIMER

Modern Marriage

"Things are so dispensable now. People live together for a while—a year, a few years, months—then they split, and they never see each other again. Then they get together with somebody else—split. Have kids—split. Then the kids never see each other. It's absolutely frightening—this incessant estrangement that's going on. People are being amputated from each other and from themselves."
—Sam Shepard; divorced with a son, he is now living with Jessica Lange, her daughter by Mikhail Baryshnikov, and their two children

A recent study suggests that premarital cohabitation increases the chance of divorce by 80 percent.

"In today's society you don't need to be married. You don't need to tidy up. Not at my age, anyway. I think I've outgrown that."
—Elizabeth Taylor, in 1990, before marrying Larry Fortensky

"The angel sent down to expel Adam and Eve was the first
Reno judge, but we are conservative; despite all thunder,
trouble, and waste of spirit, we failed to recognize him.
Now the day of natural virtue, when divorce was almost
inconceivable, is over."
>   —HERBERT GOLD, "Divorce as a Mortal Act," *Atlantic Monthly,*
>   1957

"I accept you with your body and spirit free. I do not commit
myself to the illusion forever."
>   —MODERN WEDDING VOWS, *Look* magazine, 1971

"I had a friend who was getting married, so I gave her
a subscription to *Modern Bride.* The subscription lasted longer
than the marriage."
>   —LILY TOMLIN

Median duration of marriage in the United States: seven years

Life's a Itch

The seven-year itch is really a four-year itch, according to Helen
Fisher, an anthropologist who looked at UN figures for divorce in
62 cultures. The notorious itch—when the urge to fool around may
cause husband or wife to stray—coincides with the median length
of American marriages: seven years. Fisher zeroes in on the
fourth—the year when most divorces occur. "We're replaying a
mating game that has evolved over 4 million years," Fisher says in
her book *Anatomy of Love.* "Strutting, preening, flirting, courting,
dazzling, then capturing one another. Then nesting. Then breed-

ing. Then philandering. Then abandoning the fold. Soon drunk on hope, we court anew."

A total of 1,175,000 couples divorced during the first quarter of 1990. The divorce rate in 1989 was 4.6 per 1,000 population, 2 percent above the rate for the first quarter of 1988 (4.5). 1990 statistics show another rise to 4.7 per 1,000.

"At an increasing number of weddings I note that the pews—because of divorce wars—are divided among the bride's side and the groom's side, then subdivided, say, into the groom's-father-and-new-wife's side, the bride's-mother-and-um-live-in-friend's side and . . . you get the idea."

—JUDITH VIORST

"Your basic extended family today includes your ex-husband or wife, your ex's new mate, your new mate, possibly your new mate's ex and any new mate that your new mate's ex has acquired."

—DELIA EPHRON, *Funny Sauce*

"A miserable marriage can wobble along for years until something comes along and pushes one of the people over the brink. It's usually another man or woman. For me, it was a whole production staff and camera crew."

> —PAT LOUD, *Pat Loud: A Woman's Story,* with Nora Johnson, 1974. The Loud family's breakup and divorce were chronicled in a controversial PBS documentary in the mid-1970s. In order to document the family breakup, the TV crew set up shop in their home.

Half the marriages contracted in the 1970s will not last.

"Our divorce was a protest against Vietnam."
>—Woody Allen, on his 1970 divorce from second wife, Louise Lasser

"As lovers, modern men and women may not be nearly as graceful as the Renaissance courtiers, as lusty as the rationalists, nor as sweetly eloquent as the Victorians; yet more than any of these they consider love the sine qua non of the happy life. Americans, who make more of marrying for love than any other people, also break up more of their marriages (close to 400,000 annually), but the figure reflects not so much the failure of love as the determination of people not to live without it."
>—Morton Hunt, *The Natural History of Love,* 1959

"It isn't silence you can cut with a knife anymore, it's interchange of ideas. Intelligent discussion of practically everything is what is breaking up modern marriage."
>—E. B. White

On an average day in America 6,567 couples are married; 3,197 are divorced.

"Easy divorces have just about put arguing out of business."
>—Red Skelton

53 percent of women
42 percent of men
} think divorce should be more difficult to obtain than it is now.

"Our divorce laws are more relaxed now and women are in

competition with men. Marriage is on the way out. I don't think it will exist in another hundred years."

—CARY GRANT

"The church needs to wake up and find some way to cope with divorce and women's problems."

—ANITA BRYANT

> 22 percent of Catholic women } would like to see a greater acceptance of divorce in the Catholic Church.
> 12 percent of Catholic men

"One problem is that we have no reference points. All our traditions are crumbling. Look at the Catholic Church. The only people who want to get married today are Catholic priests."

—MORTIMER FEINBERG, *Business Week,* 1975

A Vatican court ruled in August 1991 that drug addiction is a valid reason to annul a Roman Catholic marriage. The church rejects divorce but grants annulments, which effectively means the marriage never took place.

"He's certain to get the divorce vote and remember that's one in four these days."

—CLEVELAND AMORY, 1962, on Governor Rockefeller's political future following his divorce

Although several widowers have been elected to the White House, only two never-married men—Grover Cleveland, who married while in office, and lifelong bachelor James Buchanan—were elected President.

"The divorce wasn't her fault, but divorce is sort of a common thing these days, and it just happened that it happened to me."
—PETE ROSE; his ex-wife, Karolyn, got the $300,000 home in the suburbs, $72,000 in temporary alimony, $105,000 in cash, and the 1978 Rolls-Royce

"We have a long way to go as a human race. There are far more important things to think about than Donald Trump and Marla. Fifty percent of all Americans go through divorces. It's not unusual and I'm not the cause of this one."
—MARLA MAPLES

"If the divorce rate keeps increasing, part of the marriage vow will have to be changed from 'I do' to 'adieu.' "
—HY GARDNER

In 1880, 1 in 16 marriages ended in divorce.
In 1928, 1 in 6 marriages ended in divorce.
In 1991, 1 out of every 2 marriages ended in divorce.

"If our divorce rate is any indication, women aren't any better at love, sex, and commitment than men, because it takes two to tango. . . . There's a good reason for divorce!"
—RITA MAE BROWN

Love and the Law

"Divorce is a game played by lawyers."
                    —CARY GRANT, divorced four times

"We came from mud. And after 3.8 billion years of
evolution, at our core there is still mud. No one could be
a divorce lawyer and doubt that."
                    —GAVIN D'AMATO, divorce lawyer played by Danny DeVito
                    in the movie *The War of the Roses*

Multiple Wounds

Smyrna, Tennessee, lawyer John Kersey pleaded guilty to assault
and agreed to counseling and to give up his law license for five
years. A female divorce client had accused him of locking her in
his office, threatening to hit her if she did not correctly answer
questions based on schoolbook multiplication tables, and spanking
her. Eleven other clients have come forward with similar tales.

"I don't believe man is woman's natural enemy. Perhaps his lawyer is."

—SHANA ALEXANDER

"I represented everything that can go wrong.... You have to captain your own ship. Don't rely on lawyers. They can't remember to tell you everything. They're only human. And most of them are below human."

—ROXANNE PULITZER

"I believe that every accusation made on both sides in the Pulitzer case is the truth. He did it, she did it, they all did it. They should give the money to charity and sell the kids to the Arabs."

—HUNTER S. THOMPSON

"He corrupted and polluted this farm girl. He switched her from milk to champagne and finally to drugs."

—ROBERT FARISH, Roxanne Pulitzer's attorney, in his final argument in *Pulitzer* v. *Pulitzer*, 1982

"I've made so many rulings in this case. If I haven't made an error by now, I ought to get the Pulitzer Prize."

—CARL HARPER, judge on the Pulitzer divorce case, 1982

"It is better to have loved and lost, but only if you have a good lawyer."

—HERB CAEN, columnist

The Power of Attorney

Robert Howard Singer, convicted in 1982 of murdering his wife's first husband, won a new trial because his wife had a secret sexual relationship with the lawyer who defended Singer. A state Court of Appeals, ruling in a case without legal precedent, held that the "on and off affair" between attorney William C. Melcher and Judith

Singer during the trial created a conflict of interest violating Singer's right to effective counsel. Among other things, the court noted, the conflict could have influenced the lawyer to see his client convicted and imprisoned so that the affair could continue. Melcher denied any wrongdoing, saying, "These allegations remain totally unfounded and untrue. There was no conflict of any kind . . . and I devoted monumental energy to his defense."

"A lawyer is never entirely comfortable with a friendly divorce, any more than a good mortician wants to finish his job and then have the patient sit up on the table."

—JEAN KERR

"Marriage is really tough because you have to deal with feelings and lawyers."

—RICHARD PRYOR, divorced five times

"I'll chew John Tesh and his bald lawyer up for breakfast."
—JAMES WOODS, on being subpoenaed to testify in the divorce trial of John Tesh and his wife, Julie, whom Woods is now dating

"It's really lawyers that make divorces nasty. You know, if there was a nice ceremony like getting married for divorce, it'd be much better."

—JOHN LENNON, 1971

Without a Hitch

About a dozen California couples have written their own vows, gathered their friends together and told of how each had affected the other's life. This is known as a "divorce ceremony" instituted by Mountain View therapist Jean Hollands. The idea is to create a quiet moment to mark the end of a marriage and formally say good-bye. Among the brave few, half simply gathered their children and in-laws in Hollands's office. The vows usually involve promises to "release" each other, reflections on the good things about the marriage, and reassurances to children. As for the divorce ceremonies, "everyone gets invited but the lover or the new husband or wife. Plan a gentle party. Keep the ceremony itself short, no longer than 10 minutes. And explain the concept to the children and grandparents," said Hollands.

"What a holler would ensue if people had to pay the minister as much to marry them as they have to pay a lawyer to get them a divorce."

—CLAIRE TREVOR

"Consent, if mutual, saves the lawyer's fee. Consent is law enough to set you free."

—GEORGE FARQUHAR, *The Beaux' Stratagem*

" 'Will you be wanting to contest the divorce?' I asked Mrs. Davis. 'I think not,' she said calmly, 'although I suppose one of us should, for the fun of the thing. An uncontested divorce always seems to me contrary to the spirit of divorce.' "

—DONALD BARTHELME, *At the End of the Mechanical Age*

"Diana sued for divorce February of 1949. There wasn't any such thing as no-fault divorce then. You had to have one party in the wrong, you had to have a specific reason, and you had to have witnesses, which made it more unpleasant. Mental cruelty was the most innocuous accusation possible; we went for that.... Afterward, we had a beer together and watched our divorce on the evening news as we critiqued the coverage. We laughed but it wasn't funny."

—KIRK DOUGLAS

"Where divorce is allowed at all ... society demands a specific grievance of one party against the other.... The fact that marriage may be a failure spiritually is seldom taken into account."

—SUZANNE LAFOLLETTE, "The Beginnings of Emancipation," *Concerning Women*, 1926

"What starts love is looking through rose-colored glasses.
You idealize your future with this other person; you put your
best foot forward. Then real living sets in. Romance takes a
back seat to bills, job aggravations, family problems. You
focus on those things instead of cultivating your
relationship. When you plant a tree and don't water it, it dies.
So does love."

>   —MARVIN MITCHELSON, divorce and palimony lawyer, author of
>   *Made in Heaven, Settled in Court*

"They've taken all the romance out of divorce."

>   —RAOUL FELDER, New York celebrity divorce lawyer, on the changes
>   in divorce law, 1988. Felder recently sent out elegant black
>   umbrellas that opened up to reveal the message, "Sue
>   Someone You Love."

"The state has no business in the bedrooms of the nation."

>   —PIERRE ELLIOT TRUDEAU, Prime Minister of Canada, in an appeal
>   for revised divorce laws, 1968

"It's difficult to tell which gives some couples the most happiness,
the minister who marries them or the judge who divorces them."

>   —MARY WILSON LITTLE, nineteenth-century American writer

Judge-Mental

Broward County, Florida, Judge Paul Marko, in a 1990 divorce
case, forbade Marianne Price, 33, from having boyfriends over to
her house (because it was formerly joint property) but said her husband could have the "entire Dolphins cheerleading squad running
through his apartment naked" because it was "his" apartment.
Marko then advised Price to start visiting singles bars: "I've been
[in them]. I'm a single man. There are all kinds of bimbos . . . and
. . . guys running around in open shirts with eagles on their chests.
There are great guys out there." Marko said he would order Price's
house sold if she allowed a male to live there: "I don't want her all

of a sudden taking up with some nice, sweet, little blond from Norway." Marko later apologized to Price.

"The judge is so madly in love with this defendant, Bill Hurt, that we never could have gotten a fair shake. . . . If we won, I would have been shocked. . . ."

> —RICHARD GOLUB, Sandra Jennings's lawyer in her
> common-law marriage battle

"Love is generally valued at its highest during two periods in life: during the days of courting and the days in court."

> —LEE MARVIN

Pistol Packin' Papa

A man carrying two pistols opened fire during his divorce hearing at the St. Louis County Court in May 1992, killing his wife and wounding four others. Both her attorney and her husband's attorney were wounded. The gunman, Kenneth Baumruk, 53, then left the courtroom and shot a bailiff and a security guard in a hallway before being shot by two officers, police said. He was later reported to be in critical condition. Slain was Mary Baumruk, 46.

"You don't know anything about a woman until you meet her in court."

> —NORMAN MAILER, divorced five times

"Whoever said 'marriage is a 50-50 proposition' laid the foundation for more divorce fees than any other short sentence in our language."

> —AUSTIN ELLIOT; some observations on the attorney-secretary
> function, *Law Office Economics and Management,* 1964

"Why do Jewish divorces cost so much? Because they're worth it."

> —HENNY YOUNGMAN

"For a while we pondered whether to take a vacation or
get a divorce. We decided that a trip to Bermuda is over in
two weeks, but a divorce is something you always have."

—WOODY ALLEN

"Paper napkins never return from the laundry, nor love from
a trip to the law courts."

—JOHN BARRYMORE

"I wanted Claude and Paloma to have their rights for
justice. . . . I didn't want them considered bastards. . . .
When we were in love, I didn't think I would have to resort
to the law with Pablo because I thought love was stronger than
the law."

　　　—FRANÇOISE GILOT; she had two children out of wedlock with
　　　　　Pablo Picasso while he was still legally married to Olga
　　　　　Koklova

"I think it's like the S&L crisis. We'll know the end of
it in 1999."

—JONI EVANS, on divorcing Simon & Schuster chairman Richard Snyder

The Seven-Year Glitch

One of the nation's most prolonged and bitter divorce cases ended
December 16, 1991, at the Supreme Court. The couple, who dis-
puted virtually every major and minor issue during a seven-year
Los Angeles court war, finally agreed that the $3 million in fees
charged by their lawyers was excessive. Millionaires Stanley and
Dorothy Diller were the antagonists in an epic divorce case involving 110 court hearings and a marathon trial lasting 49 days. The
court reporter's transcript consumed 5,165 pages in 20 volumes
more than 6 feet high. "No amount of advice from the judge de-
terred the parties from their obsession to grind on with the litiga-
tion, without concern as to its costs or consumption of time," a

California appeals judge wrote of the case. The Dillers divorced after 28 years of marriage.

Trial Judge Robert Fainer, who approved the fee requests, described Dorothy Diller as "a frightened, bitter woman" who was "obsessed" by her belief that her husband was concealing community property. Her husband, the judge wrote, was "an avaricious, covetous, stubborn man." A lawyer, referring to a 1989 film depicting a violent divorce battle, said that the Dillers "acted out in the courtroom their own *War of the Roses*."

After living through divorce negotiations, I would advise other
women to make their own decisions. A divorce is often the
first time women ever take any control—most don't know
about insurance policies or stocks or whatever. I didn't feel
this way when the divorce began. I was very concerned that
Bruce think well of me. I thought that if I stepped quietly out
the back door he would always say what a nice girl I was.
Then I began to realize that regardless of what I took or
didn't take, he wasn't going to speak highly of me."
    —CHRYSTIE JENNER; she worked for four years while husband, Bruce
    Jenner, trained for the Olympics

Lit-Egg-Ation

The Knoxville, Tennessee, state Supreme Court upheld a man's right to refuse to become a father by way of seven embryos from his ex-wife's eggs fertilized in a test tube three and a half years before. The five-judge court ruled unanimously that privacy rights require that Junior Davis not be forced into fatherhood. After the divorce, his ex-wife offered to donate the embryos to another childless couple. If that happened, the court said, Davis "would face a lifetime of either wondering about his parental status or knowing about his parental status but having no control over it." After Davis and his wife were unable to conceive naturally, a Knoxville clinic used his sperm and her eggs to produce the embryos in December 1988. The court said the embryos were not strictly people or property, "but occupy an interim category that entitles them to special respect because of their potential for human life." They remain at the Knoxville clinic, frozen in liquid nitrogen. Davis, 33, now lives in Maryville, Tennessee. Mary Sue Davis Stowe, 31, lives in Titusville, Florida.

"While in most states the divorce laws are the same for men and women, they never can bear equally upon both while all the property earned during the marriage belongs wholly to the husband."

> —SUSAN B. ANTHONY, "The Status of Women, Past, Present and Future," *The Arena,* 1897

"What I'm doing in this car flying down these screaming highways is getting my tail to Juarez so I can legally rid myself of the crummy son-of-a-bitch who promised me a tomorrow like a yummy fruitcake and delivered instead wilted lettuce, rotted cucumber, a garbage of a life."

> —ANNE RICHARDSON ROIPHE, *Long Division,* 1972

"I told myself I had to be Job, I had to be patient, but at the same time I was in court with the worst kind of mudslinging divorce."

> —BEVERLY JOHNSON, fashion model

"Chapter Two"

"I think Neil thought I was out of my mind. We'd been through all these charming luncheons and meetings, drawing up the papers—Magna Carta! Neil had a stack this high of what he wanted. I said, 'O.K., now let's put down what I want.' The lawyers were stunned. But I got my one line. The reason I did it was because I didn't want him observing the relationship. I wanted him to live it. I thought if I took away his ability to write about it, he might treat it differently."

> —DIANE LANDER, on preparing her prenuptial agreement with Neil Simon. They divorced in 1988 and remarried in 1990.

"And I, after two failures, convinced that women were
stronger and more cynical than men, was wary of love.
I tried to love her, but I was going through a temporary crisis
of misogyny, and although an affectionate person by nature,
I was sometimes cruel. She took the rough with the smooth
with apparent serenity. I never noticed that she was quietly
sharpening her claws. One day I found myself in a lawyer's
chambers in the Boulevard Saint-Michel drawing up a marriage
contract. Her parents were discussing a set of kitchen
utensils, which was to be retained by one of us in the event
of death or divorce, and I was signing the papers without bothering
to read them, convinced that this kind of thing had died out
with Balzac."

—ROGER VADIM, on ex-wife Catherine Deneuve

"I'd have to be with somebody who I could ask for one [a
prenuptial agreement]. They'd have to be not insulted if I asked
for one—bottom line."

—MADONNA

"I never saw a prenuptial agreement yet that didn't wind up
in a divorce."

—MARVIN MITCHELSON, palimony lawyer

Places in the Heart

"America is the land of permanent waves and impermanent wives."

—BRENDAN BEHAN

"American husbands are the best in the world; no other husbands are so generous to their wives, or can be so easily divorced."

—ELINOR GLYN

"Marriage is hardly a thing one can do now and then, except in America."

—OSCAR WILDE

In 1981 a record 1.21 million divorces took place in America, with California leading the way with 133,578.

In January 1970, the state of California put no-fault divorce on the map. The law signed by then-governor Ronald Reagan, was hailed as the first step toward making divorce rational, equitable, modern, quick, and civilized.

"In California, marriage is a felony."
> —JOANNE ASTRAL, *Evening at the Improv,* NBC-TV, 1982

"Hollywood brides keep the bouquets and throw away the grooms."
> —GROUCHO MARX

"In some countries being president is just an honorary position—like being a husband in Hollywood."
> —EARL WILSON

"There are basically two types of exercise in Hollywood these days: jogging and helping a recently divorced friend move."
> —ROBERT WAGNER

> The traditional family—a married couple—continues to decline. Nationally, just 55.1 percent of households were married-couple families, down from the 60.2 percent mark in 1980. The percentage declined in every state. The steepest drop was in Arizona, which fell from 62.2 percent in 1980 to 54.6 percent in 1990. California showed the smallest decline, going from 55.2 percent in 1980 to 52.7 percent in 1990.

"In New York State, they have a strange law that says you can't get a divorce unless you can prove adultery. And that is weird because the Ten Commandments say: 'Thou shalt not commit adultery,' but New York State says you have to."
> —WOODY ALLEN

"A New York divorce is in itself a diploma of virtue."
> —EDITH WHARTON, *The Other Two*

"I am alone here in New York, no longer a we."
> —ELIZABETH HARDWICK, on her divorce, *Sleepless Nights*

"My husband wanted a room of his own: He wanted it in Pittsburgh."

—PHYLLIS DILLER

Couples in the New South—states including Georgia, North Carolina, South Carolina, and the southern parts of Virginia, West Virginia, Maryland, and Delaware—are less likely than people in other parts of the nation to be divorced in the next five years.

According to a 1992 poll:
71 percent of West Virginians are in love.
93 percent would marry their spouse again.
64 percent say love is the most important reason for marriage.

There are currently 6.2 divorces for every 1,000 population in Florida. The national figure is 4.7 for every 1,000 population.

"Once you've met the women, you can see why the men have died or run away."

—HELEN BOEHM, American socialite/businesswoman, on Palm Beach marriages

"In Palm Beach you do not ever get divorced during the season."

—CHARLOTTE CURTIS

"The London season is entirely matrimonial; people are either hunting for husbands or hiding from them."

—OSCAR WILDE

Royal Splits

"She is the best thing in my life."

—Prince Andrew

"I love his wit, his charm, his looks. I worship him."

—Sarah Ferguson, 1986

1992

March 18   Prince Andrew and his wife, the former Sarah Ferguson, prepare to announce their separation after about five and a half years of marriage.

March 19   Fergie, 32, reportedly pleads for Queen Elizabeth II's permission to leave her husband (the couple must seek permission to part from the queen under the Royal Marriages Act of 1772). Apparently, all parties are now in accord, and the duchess will have custody of daughters Beatrice, 3, and Eugenie, 2, but the prince will have full access to them. What happens to Fergie's title and how much money she'll get is undecided.

March 20   Buckingham Palace confirms the breakup of the marriage of Prince Andrew and Sarah, Duchess of York and author of *Budgie the Little Helicopter.* "The knives are out for Fergie at the palace," BBC reporter Paul Reynolds says after a news briefing there. According to royal insider Charlie Jacoby, the palace "will now proceed to destroy Fergie's character to prevent her from publishing her memoirs, or embarrassing the palace."

March 22   The duchess is now being made aware of the
                      full consequences of her split from Andrew.
                      The Friargate Museum in York, northern En-
                      gland, dumps a waxwork of Fergie from its
                      royal display. She joins other royal spouses pre-
                      viously eliminated from the exhibit, including
                      Princess Anne's husband, Mark Phillips, who
                      was melted down and turned into a clown, and
                      Princess Margaret's husband, Lord Snowdon,
                      who was turned into George Bush.

"I like her too much to go out with her. She doesn't deserve
that."

> —SYLVESTER STALLONE, about rumors that he
> and the Duchess of York are an item.

1992

                      The Vatican announces that Princess Caroline
                      of Monaco's request for an annulment of her
                      marriage to Philippe Junot is still under study.
                      She and Junot divorced in 1980, but an annul-
                      ment would allow her to remarry in the Church.
                      Three years after divorcing Junot, she married
                      an Italian businessman in a 1983 civil cere-
                      mony. He was killed in a speedboat crash in
                      October 1990.

April 14   Princess Anne is divorcing Mark Phillips. It is
                      only the second divorce in the inner circle of
                      the royal family since the 16th century, when
                      King Henry VIII spurned four of his six wives,
                      beheading two. (The other divorce was granted
                      to the queen's sister, Princess Margaret, who
                      ended her marriage to photographer Lord
                      Snowdon in 1978.)

Some royal facts about Anne and Mark:

- At a party in 1968, Anne meets Mark, a former officer in the exclusive Dragoon Guards who nonetheless lacks the blue-blood pedigree and aristocratic background once expected of royal spouses.
- November 1973, they marry in a lavish wedding in Westminster Abbey.
- 1977, the couple gives birth to Peter.
- 1981, daughter Zara is born, after which Anne and Mark live virtually separate lives.
- 1989, allegations that Anne is involved in a romance with royal equerry, Timothy Laurence.
- Months later, the couple officially separate.
- 1991, a New Zealand equestrienne names Mark as the father of her 5-year-old daughter.
- April 1992, Princess Anne and Mark Phillips divorce after a two-year separation.
- May 1992, Princess Anne announces her engagement to a naval officer with whom she has been linked since 1989. The 41-year-old princess reportedly has talked to her parents about plans to marry 37-year-old Timothy Laurence.

June 8   Britain is abuzz over Princess Diana's attempted suicide due to the state of her marriage to Prince Charles, and a recent book claims that she took an overdose of pills in 1986. Another book claims the princess tried to kill herself, not once, but *five* times early in her marriage. Diana flung herself down some stairs, slashed at her wrists with a razor blade, cut her chest and thighs with a knife and threw herself at a glass cabinet, Andrew Morton writes in *Diana—Her True Story*. "Another time she cut herself with the serrated edge of a lemon slicer," he says.

June 13

"No one dragged you along to marry a prince. . . . But if you choose that path, you simply can't foul up the monarchy."—Barbara Cartland, the 91-year-old romance writer, giving her step-granddaughter, Princess Diana, some advice about her marriage to Charles

June 23

Prince Charles reportedly believes Princess Diana is behind the book that alleges she tried to commit suicide because of a loveless marriage. London's daily *Sun* reports that Charles refuses to read *Diana—Her True Story*. "When I hear what is in the book, I can hear my wife's voice saying exactly the same words," he says. He feels Diana's cooperation is "a total betrayal." The paper says Charles insists on maintaining a dignified silence, but friends urge him to talk openly and "deal with the matter."

July 2

After 10 years of deliberations, a Vatican court annuls the first marriage of Princess Caroline of Monaco.

July 7

Prince Charles's friends say Princess Diana is "seriously unbalanced" and has distorted the truth about the couple's marriage because of her illness, a newspaper reports. "The fact is, he has spent the past 11 years living with a seriously unbalanced wife," says an article in *Today* newspaper by royals watcher Penny Junor. "The princess is not the only one who has been miserable and lonely and disillusioned by an empty marriage," the article continues. The article also defends Charles as a father, saying he adores his children but Diana thwarts his attempts to see them.

It's Prince Charles's fault, according to a survey of Britons. More people blamed him (35 percent) than Princess Diana (16 percent) for the shaky state of the royal marriage. The Harris Research poll also found 24 percent of those asked think the couple should separate, 24 percent think they should divorce and 42 percent vote for staying together.

In 1992, one out of every three British marriages ended in divorce.

"I sleep better when Bella is in Washington. I sleep even better when she's in Cambodia."

—MARTIN ABZUG, husband of Bella Abzug

In 1990, the percentage of married-couple families ranged from as low as 25.3 percent in the District of Columbia to 64.8 percent in Utah. Florida's 54.4 percent was slightly below average.

The District of Columbia has the highest proportion of single-parent families at 23.6 percent—almost the same as the District's percentage of married couples. North Dakota has the lowest percentage, with just 9.9 percent. Florida was average, with 14 percent.

"I married beneath me. All women do."

—NANCY, LADY ASTOR, divorced in 1903 and remarried three years later to Waldorf Astor; her divorce was a source of embarrassment in her later career, when she became a vigorous opponent of divorce

"I tended to place my wife under a pedestal."

—Woody Allen

"A woman's place is in the wrong."

—James Thurber

"A woman's place is in the stove."

—Mort Sahl

"A woman's place is in the bedroom."

—Ferdinand Marcos

Calling It Quits

The following number of states consider these acts grounds for divorce:

37	Bigamy
31	Impotence
30	Adultery
30	Desertion
29	Cruelty
28	Insanity
26	Felony conviction, imprisonment
25	Separation
23	Alcoholism
17	Nonsupport
14	Drug addiction
13	Unknown pregnancy at marriage

Minnesota and Missouri recognize very few grievances as grounds for divorce. Alabama and West Virginia allow the most.

The United States is at the top of the world's divorce charts. Compared with the 4.7 per 1,000 rate in the United States, French marriages disintegrate at a more sedate 2.0, and it's 1.4 in Japan.

"He took me by storm. I was on a flying carpet—serenades in Venice, baccarat in Nice, marriage in Las Vegas—but when the carpet landed, bang! All he wanted to do was exhibit me to the Shah of Iran or some important businessman. I hated it. We were never alone."
> —BRIGITTE BARDOT, on her divorce from Gunther Sachs, a German playboy/industrialist

The European Community is looking into ways of simplifying divorce recognition within its 12 member countries. At present, for example, a divorce is not recognized in Italy without a sworn translation authenticated by an Italian consulate, and fresh proceedings in Italy.

Divorce is banned in Chile, but second marriages are common. Marriages in Latin America can be easily annulled by finding—or inventing—a technical flaw in the marriage papers. This system has long avoided a direct confrontation with the powerful Roman Catholic Church over divorce, while allowing people to live the way they want to live. Now, as Chile's civilian government debates a divorce law, some women in second marriages have been the most strident opponents of change.

Outlawing the In-Laws

"My mother-in-law broke up my marriage. One day my wife came home early from work and found us in bed together."

—LENNY BRUCE

Going Nuts

A 33-year-old Virginia Beach man told police that he had mistaken his mother-in-law for a large raccoon when he killed her with a hatchet in his garage in 1981. He said that after he hit her once, he realized it was his mother-in-law and then he hit her again. "I snapped . . . or something," he said.

"Distrust all mothers-in-law. They are completely unscrupulous in what they say in court. The wife's mother is always more prejudiced against the husband than even the most ill-treated wife. If I had my way, I am afraid I would abolish all mothers-in-law entirely."

—SIR GEOFFREY WRANGHAM, British High Court Justice and specialist in divorce cases, 1960

"I said to my mother-in-law, 'My house is your house.'
She said, 'Get the hell off my property.' "

—JOAN RIVERS

"I'll tell you, Erica, the longer I'm married to you, the more
you sound like my mother."

—*AN UNMARRIED WOMAN,* faithless husband Michael Murphy
to Jill Clayburgh

"I never liked him from the beginning."

—JOE COLLINS, Joan's father on ex-husband Peter Holm

"I felt like a peasant trying to date the queen's daughter."

—MIKE TYSON on ex-mother-in-law Ruth Roper

21 percent of women think their husband gets along
better with her parents than with his; 14 percent of
men think their wife gets along better with his parents
than with hers.

"We are always studiously polite to each other, but it is rather
like a volcano ready to burst at any moment."

—JENNIE CHURCHILL, on her mother-in-law, Frances Churchill

"When a couple decide to divorce, they should inform both
sets of parents before having a party and telling their friends.
This is not only courteous but practical. Parents may be very
willing to pitch in with comments, criticism and malicious
gossip of their own to help the divorce along."

—P. J. O'ROURKE

Theory of Relativity

Mohammed Abdel Rahman, 29, leaped to his death from the balcony of his hotel on his wedding night in Cairo in 1987 after he discovered that his mother-in-law tricked him into marrying the uglier of her two daughters. Rahman had entrusted wedding details to the mother-in-law when he was sent out of the country on business shortly before the wedding, and she slipped the other daughter's name onto the dotted line.

"The luckiest man was Adam—he had no mother-in-law."

—SHOLEM ALEICHEM

The Case
Against Divorce

"The worst reconciliation is preferable to the best divorce."

—Cervantes

"The absurd is essentially a divorce. It is neither one nor
the other of the compared elements. It is born of their
confrontation."

—Albert Camus, *The Myth of Sisyphus*

"So many persons think divorce a panacea for every ill,
who find out, when they try it, that the remedy is worse
than the disease."

—Dorothy Dix, *Her Book*

"The divorced person is like a man with a black patch over
one eye: He looks rather dashing but the fact is that he
has been through a maiming experience."

—Jo Coudert, *Advice from a Failure*

> 81 percent of women ⎫ think the good of a marriage
> 79 percent of men   ⎰ exceeds the bad.
>
> 8 percent of women ⎫ think the bad of a marriage ex-
> 5 percent of men   ⎰ ceeds the good.

"The divorce is like a side dish that nobody remembers having ordered."

—ALEXANDER KING, *I Should Have Kissed Her More*

Near Miss

Mrs. America almost lacked one accoutrement essential to a successful reign: a husband. Pageant officials told Jill Scott, the 1991 Mrs. America, that her divorce plans conflicted with the concept. Mrs. Scott, 33, separated from husband G. E. Scott of Scottsdale, Arizona, in September 1990, just months before winning the title. As it turned out, she made it through her tenure as Mrs. America without officially filing for divorce. If she signed the papers before her reign ended, "we'd both have exes. She'd have an ex-husband and we'd have an ex-Mrs. America," said the pageant's president, David Marmel.

"A divorce is like an amputation; you survive, but there's less of you."

—MARGARET ATWOOD

"Divorce is not always in error, but always in error is what the divorced dream they will do next."

—ARNOLD WHITBY, American writer

"Divorces as well as marriages can fail."

—MAURICE MERLEAU-PONTY, *Signs*

Life After Divorce

> 48 percent of divorced women think their husbands were happier after the divorce; 40 percent of divorced men think that of their wives.

"He's looking old. That makes me feel great."
> —FAYE HACKMAN, upon seeing Gene, husband of 30 years, on a *Joan Rivers* segment on life after divorce

Mighty Python and the Holey Box

Jacqueline Pearl Pointer, 43, was indicted in Birmingham, Alabama, in March 1991 on charges of sending a live poisonous snake through the mail to John Temerson, her former husband. Temerson called police when the box with holes but no return address, was delivered.

"A wife lasts only for the length of the marriage, but an ex-wife is there for the rest of your life."
> —JIM SAMUELS, stand-up comedian

"[My marriage] wasn't all that great to begin with. . . . I
will survive—I'm unsinkable."
>   —ANITA BRYANT, after divorcing Bob Green in 1980. In 1990,
>   she married Charlie Dry—her childhood sweetheart.

78 percent of divorced women⎱ were happier after the
65 percent of divorced men ⎰ divorce.

The Naked Truth

A Marietta, Georgia, man was ordered to pay his ex-wife $225,000
for sending a nude photograph of her to a men's magazine without
her permission or knowledge. A jury ordered Jennings Gordon, 50,
to pay the money, saying he violated Susan Hudson's privacy when
he not only sent the nude photos to *Gallery* magazine but also sent
copies of the magazine to her employer and mother. Gordon admitted forging Hudson's name on a model release for *Gallery*'s 1985
"Girl Next Door Amateur Erotic Photo Contest," but told jurors,
"This is the woman I love. I cannot explain, nor do I know why I
did these things."

Call of the Child

Laurel Vutano, 33, a Pinellas County, Florida, teacher, was suspended for being affectionate with her boyfriend in front of her
second-grade class and for encouraging her students (with 50-cent
offers) to make obnoxious phone calls to her boyfriend's estranged
wife. The wife reported "many" calls "from little voices."

Stolen Passes

Two unidentified high-school seniors told police they burglarized the home of a teacher's estranged wife in exchange for passing grades. Peter Mayall Galloway and his wife were separated in 1990, court records show. The students led police to some of the stolen property and said Galloway had given them a map of his wife's apartment in Quinlan, Texas, and a list of items to take. They said Galloway told them, "You do this for me, and I'll see to it that [you pass]."

"There is no fury like an ex-wife searching for a new lover."
—CYRIL CONNOLLY

55 percent of women } who have close friends who
45 percent of men { went through a divorce think the wife was happier after the divorce.

"Since I've been divorced, there has always been a man in my life. I enjoy male company enormously.... I cannot imagine my life without a man. I think when I'm 90 I'll still have a fella."

—ANN LANDERS

"Mine was not a terribly painful, miserable, rotten divorce with animosity and anxiety. I just knew that my life was going to have to change and I was determined to make it better. The divorce was going to improve my life. And it did."

—ANN LANDERS

"I'm enjoying my new life—I'm even dating. It's delicious. It's scary. It's lonely. But it's right."

—MEREDITH BAXTER-BIRNEY, after her 15-year marriage to David Birney

"A lot of Frank rubbed off. I'm not as insecure and I've learned about the force called power."

— MIA FARROW, after her divorce from Frank Sinatra in 1969

> who have friends who went
> **38 percent of women** } through a divorce think the
> **46 percent of men** } husband was happier after the
> divorce.

"I don't miss having sex with her; I don't even miss her cooking. I miss our being able to laugh together. . . ."

— ORSON BEAN, on ex-wife

"At my age, it's very difficult to find any kind of romantic involvement because most men are either gay or married."

— BEA ARTHUR, 12 years after her divorce from film director Gene Saks

"I wish that at my age I had made a marriage work. I wish I had a healthy husband about seventy—a companion who liked to go to the theater."

— SHELLEY WINTERS, divorced three times

"If I can get through this year, I can get through anything. I'm still functioning under all this pressure. I'm more confident than I've ever been—I guess."

— PENNY MARSHALL, after her nine-year marriage to Rob Reiner

The Bonds of Matrimony

John Alvin Jackson of Trenton, South Carolina, admitted giving his estranged wife to another man to settle a $200 debt because he was "red hot mad" at her. After getting her to go with him under the pretense of spending a long weekend at a lake to try to reconcile their marriage, he suggested they stop by Frank William Yeck's place in Grovetown, Georgia, to pick up a Bible. There, Jackson handed her over. Yeck placed her in bondage and forced her to participate in various sexual activities before she escaped the next day.

"It wasn't exactly a divorce. I was traded."

—TIM CONWAY

He Said . . .
She Said

"At least I can say I went two rounds with the best light heavyweight the British ever sent over."
> —NORMAN MAILER, on ex-wife number three, Lady Jeanne Campbell

"Here I married this great and powerful writer, and all we ever did was go to dinner with his mother."
> —LADY JEANNE CAMPBELL, on Norman Mailer

54 percent of wives
60 percent of husbands
} say they spend enough time with their spouses

"I think Jane takes her work too seriously. Jane says she loves me but is no longer 'in love' with me and says this is a fine distinction. I think she is nervous, despondent and therefore feels our life together has become humdrum."
> —RONALD REAGAN, on Jane Wyman

"We're through, we're finished and it's my fault."
> —JANE WYMAN, on Ronald Reagan

"She's one of the great people in the world. She's a remarkable woman. She's just one of those people who come along in life every once in a while. She's a much bigger person than she was raised to believe.... It took us three years to split up. We'd look at each other and say, 'We love each other, so what's wrong?' Turns out we just work much better as friends than spouses."

—PETER HORTON, after his seven-year marriage to Michelle Pfeiffer

"I hate to admit it. I don't believe in women being saved by men, but I think it was true. I was very lucky."

—MICHELLE PFEIFFER, on being rescued by Peter Horton from a vegetarian cult when she was 22

"No man that loved his wife gave her more freedom than I gave you."

—PETTER LINDSTROM, to Ingrid Bergman

"Please, Petter, I realize that to break up a marriage is a tragic thing, but it hasn't killed anyone. I thought it quite amusing that in the four months I have gone, Paulette Goddard had divorced, Ann Todd in England divorced her husband after twelve years and married the director David Lean, Viveca Lindfors, Ginger Rogers, Joan Fontaine, and Alida Valli have sued for divorce. Don't think this is the end of the world, your life, and your work.... It is only for you to take the first step which naturally is the most difficult: to realize and agree that our marriage is finished."

—INGRID BERGMAN, in a letter to Petter Lindstrom

"After all is said and done, it's usually the wife who has said it, and the husband who has done it."

—SAMMY KAYE

70 percent of women ⎱ say poor communication is a
59 percent of men ⎰ cause of divorce.

"I was led to believe I wasn't responsible for birth control.
It was a communications situation there."
> —STEVE GARVEY, on impregnating a number of would-be
> brides, 1989

"Look at the path of destruction he has left, and he's still smiling
at the cameras. Steve is now blaming the women involved,
and I find that appalling ... the guy is a sociopath. He
doesn't have the same level of conscience as most men."
> —CYNDY GARVEY, on ex-husband Steve Garvey whom she divorced
> in 1981. In 1989, she was ordered to serve five days in jail
> for violating a child visitation order

"Myra's still up and going, and she still looks as good as
she did back then. I don't like that. She should have aged some.
She looks just like she did when she was twelve. I wonder
if she can screw any better."
> —JERRY LEE LEWIS, on ex-wife Myra Lewis

"Everyone that's walked into Jerry's life has either become
a tragedy, a fatality, or a disruption."
> —MYRA LEWIS, on ex-husband Jerry Lee Lewis

"I watched this incredibly optimistic, bubbling, energetic,
beautiful redhead day after day. I was a happily married man
at the time. But the more I saw her, the more I became fascinated
by her."
> —GERALDO RIVERA

"I was 23. He was my boss.... I was very worried about my

job. Geraldo didn't have to worry about his job. He had to
worry about his marriage."

—C. C. Dyer, object of Geraldo's passion, now his wife

"I like Ivana a lot. Ivana loves me. What Ivana wants is to
have everything work. That's an easy solution in one sense.
I'll never say a bad thing about Ivana, but people grow
apart and as they grow apart you have to make the decision:
Do you stay or do you not stay? I'll always treat Ivana great."

—Donald Trump, 1990

"I never like to see a family fall apart. There's so much
hurt. It couldn't be saved. . . . I tried. I really tried."

—Ivana Trump, 1991

"One night with her was worth a lifetime."

—Roger Vadim, on ex-wife Brigitte Bardot,
Memoirs of the Devil, 1975

"I despise him."

—Brigitte Bardot, on ex-husband Roger Vadim

"She saw life with me as a cake called happiness that she
could eat day and night, winter and summer, awake or
asleep. She used to sulk in the morning when I had not been
nice to her in her dreams. This obsession with happiness was
to become critical with Brigitte. It was inevitable that sooner
or later she would hold me responsible for the fact that
the world did not fit the image of her fantasies and that she
would one day look for a more gifted creator."

—Roger Vadim, on ex-wife Brigitte Bardot

"He snored in his sleep and walked about the flat half the
day in his suspenders, and worst of all, he had become more
of a brother than a lover."

—Brigitte Bardot, on first husband Roger Vadim

"I was thinking, 'Man this is the greatest thing since sliced cheese' and she was thinking, 'How am I gonna get rid of this guy?' "

—SONNY BONO

"It would be very difficult to be Mr. Cher. I was with one man for 11 years and it wasn't that much fun. I can't see staying in there to say, 'I'm a martyr, what a good job I did.' If I'd stayed with Sonny, I wouldn't have had Elijah, wouldn't be an actress, wouldn't be a woman. God, I'd be dead."

—CHER

"Her priorities shifted when she started filming *Foul Play,* and our kids were sort of left as number-two priority."

—BILL HUDSON; Goldie Hawn's ex-husband fought for joint custody of their two children

"My priorities have always been the family. That's where I sprout from. That's where my happiness is. If I'm not happy there, other things don't help. I like that grounding."

—GOLDIE HAWN

"Relationships wear out and come to an end, just like shows."

—GRANT TINKER, TV executive, on divorce from Mary Tyler Moore in 1980

"Grant wasn't just my best friend, he was my only friend."

—MARY TYLER MOORE, on her divorce from TV executive Grant Tinker after a 12-year marriage

> 73 percent of wives } say their spouses are their
> 80 percent of husbands } best friends.

"No, no, I'm not his friend, I'm his wife."

—DIANE KEATON, from the movie *Shoot the Moon*

"It was hard to find time or reason to be together. We had become familiar strangers, helpless to prevent our relationship's slide from intense romance into even easy companionship. Whatever emotions or thought we once had in common had been fogged over and lost. . . . I was not the object of anyone's pity. In fact, it looked as though I was the cheery, faithless cad who behaved as he wished within certain socially prescribed bounds of behavior. Whereas, with a poignant and resigned half-smile, Joan Crawford Fairbanks seemed the dedicated, hardworking, utterly devoted, and long-suffering wife."

—Douglas Fairbanks, Jr.; Crawford and Fairbanks divorced in 1934. His second wife died in 1988 and he remarried in July 1991.

"He was trying to prove something, that he was as good a man as his father. I was his best audience, but that wasn't enough."

—Joan Crawford, on divorce from Douglas Fairbanks, Jr.

"Don't let the press feel too bad for her; Chrystie will come away from this thing financially set for the rest of her life."

—Bruce Jenner, on divorce from Chrystie Jenner

"I was supposed to supply absolutely everything emotionally, physically and financially. . . . My heart goes out to all the women who have committed themselves to support their men for . . . years."

—Chrystie Jenner, divorced from Bruce Jenner in 1980

"She's a nice lady, and I still love her very much."

—Lee Majors, after giving ex-wife Farrah Fawcett-Majors their $2.5 million Bel Air mansion

"I don't like to take shit from anybody, my lover, my parents, my friends. I don't want anybody telling me what to think or what to do."

—Farrah Fawcett-Majors, on divorcing Lee Majors after a seven-year marriage. She now lives with Lee's old friend Ryan O'Neal and their son.

23 percent of divorced women $\Big\}$ 40 percent of divorced men say that their marriages might have been successful if they and their spouses had tried harder to make the marriage work.

In the Ring with Mike and Robin: Mike Tyson v. Robin Givens

Mike Tyson first noticed Robin Givens while watching television. He arranged for a dinner date in 1987 and eventually, on February 7, 1988, Tyson, 21, married 23-year-old Robin Givens. Just months before their wedding, Tyson said, "I am never going to get married. These women are all just after my money. If I wasn't rich and famous, they wouldn't want no part of me, and I know it."

Soon after they were married, they bought a $4.5 million, 30-room mansion on 15 wooded acres in Bernardsville, New Jersey. In October, after a tumultuous eight-month marriage, Givens filed a petition demanding a divorce. She also asked the judge to issue a temporary restraining order against Tyson to keep him at least 1,000 yards away from her L.A. home, the ABC studios, and from her mother. Eight days later, Tyson filed a petition for divorce. He asked the judge to annul the marriage because Robin had tricked him into it by claiming she was pregnant.

The Gloves Are Off

In Givens's affidavit, she wrote, "Mike had, throughout our marriage, been violent and physically abusive and prone to unprovoked rages of violence and destruction. . . . The most recent incident in which I was physically terrorized by Michael occurred on October 2, 1988. [The Sunday after a *20/20* interview.] I was awakened by Michael's hitting about my body and my head with his closed fist and open hand. . . . He started throwing dishes and liquor bottles at me, and he hit me with one dish which shattered all over me. . . . Michael has repeatedly hit me, threw things at me, threatened to kill me, and kill my mother."

To these claims, Tyson said that if he beat his wife, "she'd disintegrate."

At one point, Tyson admitted his aggressions. "This is a situation in which I'm dealing with my illness. . . . She tolerates my shit and I love my wife," he said. But Givens couldn't take it for long. "It's been torture. It's been pure hell," she said. "It's been worse than anything I could possibly imagine. I'm talking about every day it's been some kind of battle, some kind of fight. . . . He gets out of control, throwing, screaming."

Tyson had his own Givens gripes. "She treats me like she's so much better than me," Tyson said. "At 21, I'm the heavyweight champion of the world, but she never lets me forget she was going to medical school and only dropped out to become a TV star and make lots of money."

On Valentine's Day in 1989, Tyson and Givens flew to the Dominican Republic for a divorce.

Givens said, "Michael can have his divorce. I never married Michael for his money. Therefore this represents no loss for me. At the cost of protecting him, I believe I sacrificed my marriage. I never wanted anything for myself."

In the end, Tyson kept his fortune and the New Jersey mansion. Givens walked away with $2 million in jewelry that Tyson reportedly gave her during the marriage. She also drove away with a few automobiles and the money she had during the marriage.

"She manipulated me," Tyson said. "Now it turns out she was lying when she said she didn't want anything from me. . . . I gave her love—and then she stabbed me in the back."

Since the Tyson-Givens divorce, Tyson was sued for fondling a young woman in a Manhattan disco. The victim demanded $2.5 million, but received $100 instead. And in September 1991, he was indicted for raping an 18-year-old beauty pageant contestant.

In February 1992, Tyson was convicted and sentenced to six years in prison.

Famous Last Words

"He called me for a divorce on the phone. . . . He said, 'This will only take a minute.' "
> —Angie Dickinson, on ex-husband Burt Bacharach, 1989

"She just tried to ruin me and destroy me. Not only did she want to take my money, but she wanted to ruin me, embarrass me, take my manhood away, and that was evil."
> —Mike Tyson, on ex-wife Robin Givens

"[He gave me] no respect, no trust, no affection, no love life, no recognition as a worthwhile human being."
> —Anita Bryant, on ex-husband Bob Green

"She's totally dominated by a man who never read a book in his life."
> —Robert Silberstein, Diana Ross's ex-husband, on Berry Gordy

"He used to grab me in his arms, hold me close—and tell me how wonderful he was."
> —Shelley Winters, on ex-husband Vittorio Gassman

"She was just like a parakeet on Benzedrine. You couldn't stop her."

> —GEORGE HAMILTON, on ex-wife Alana, who was later divorced from Rod Stewart

"He was like a parent to me. Come to think of it, it's like having to deal with your mother—so, for me, it's like going through life having *two* mothers. He could be really, really fabulous and he could be really, really . . . bad."

> —CHER, on Sonny

"I wish her fair roads and good weather. The only thing I would ask for is, 'Be successful but don't make me a victim of it.'"

> —SONNY BONO

"Sonny was the boss of the marriage, like Benito Mussolini ruled Italy."

> —CHER

"I think I married Gregory because I was tired of having someone tell me what to do. Then I chose someone who couldn't even tell himself what to do."

> —CHER, on ex-husband Gregg Allman

"I like folding Sean's underwear. I like mating socks. You know what I love? I love taking the lint out of the screen."

> —MADONNA, on what she misses most about ex-husband Sean Penn

Brief Encounter

In June 1991, a lawyer won a $3,000 settlement against a JC Penney store in Newport, Oregon, over an underwear purchase. The man claimed that after he wore the shorts for the first time, a tag ("Inspected by No. 12") stuck to his penis so firmly that he could not remove it. After soapy water and rubbing alcohol failed, he went to a doctor, who removed the sticker with an adhesive dissolver. That caused a rash, however, and when it disappeared, it left a scar in the shape of the sticker. The settlement compensated him for lost work time and for marital strife.

"I feel like my life with him has been a huge chess game, and that I've won. He's got all the money, but he didn't end up with the appearance that he wanted, that perfect person who helped the Boy Scouts. I had no choice. I could have continued to protect his name, but I would have been a martyr."
—RAYNOMA SINGLETON, on ex-husband Berry Gordy

"He kept telling me that French was a dead language."
—CATHERINE DENEUVE, on divorcing British fashion photographer David Bailey

"I gave my beauty and my youth to men. . . . What attracts me most in a man is his absence."
—BRIGITTE BARDOT, divorced three times

Costello: My daddy told me never to fall in love with a woman with beautiful legs. She might walk out on you.
Abbott: A woman with lousy legs might walk out, too.
Costello: Yeah, but who cares?

"[He] doesn't want the divorce but at this point this is the only thing he can give her."
—JIM TOMS, Jim Bakker's attorney

"It could have been a lot worse. They could have sentenced me to spend the rest of my life with Martha Mitchell."
—JOHN MITCHELL, on his 1975 Watergate conviction

"I was married once. I haven't seen her in many years. The great earthquake and fire of 1906 destroyed the marriage certificate. There's no legal proof. Which proves that earthquakes aren't all bad."

> —W. C. FIELDS, 1932; he married showgirl Harriet Hughes in
> 1900. They lived together for seven years, had a son,
> separated, and never reconciled.

"To Patti, whose love, patience and wisdom never diminished while waiting for me to grow up."

> —JERRY LEWIS, in a 1971 book dedication to now ex-wife Patti
> Lewis

"Now there's a lot of Catholics in this country who think I'm a real motherfucker because I dropped my wife of thirty-six years. When I tell you I've lived three lifetimes, I'm not being facetious."

> —JERRY LEWIS

"It's very difficult being married to Joan of Arc."

> —ROGER VADIM, on ex-wife Jane Fonda

"Why is it that when married couples separate, they so often tend to blame each other for the very qualities that attracted them to each other in the first place?"

> —SYDNEY J. HARRIS

"Ernestine was the sweetest person I ever met in my life. If I was going to marry again, I would marry Ernestine. I wouldn't marry nobody else now even if they had diamond toenails and ruby eyeballs."

> —LITTLE RICHARD, on his ex-wife

"I wonder, 'Why exchange an imperfect husband, whose failings I can deal with, for an imperfect stranger?' "

> —PENNY MARSHALL

"Our marriage would have lasted if Jason had changed his ways."

> —LAUREN BACALL, on divorce from Jason Robards

"Don't ask him what time it is or he'll tell you how to make a watch."

> —JANE WYMAN, on ex-husband Ronald Reagan

"I said I love her and was sorry for all the crap I said about her. . . . I said, 'You're a helluva gal—you just didn't make a good wife for my son.' "

> —JACKIE STALLONE, to ex-daughter-in-law Brigitte Nielsen

"I was just wrong for him, as wonderful as he was."

> —ANGIE DICKINSON, on her first divorce from college football
> star Gene Dickinson

"The bad thing about my relationship with Paul was that we were similar animals. Where there should be a flower and a gardener, we were two flowers. In the bright sun. Wilting."

> —CARRIE FISHER, on divorce from Paul Simon

"Well, there is nothing to say about that except that it's over. Period."

> —LAUREN BACALL, on her divorce from Jason Robards
> after an eight-year marriage

"John Donne, Anne Donne, Un-done."

> —JOHN DONNE, in a letter to his wife, c. 1600

"If you were well and we were both younger our marriage would be over."

> —ANN FLEMING, wife of novelist Ian Fleming, in a letter, 1962

"When people on the social scene start to gossip, it can destroy a marriage faster than a fire can race through dry timber. It probably wouldn't destroy a marriage that's pretty solid. But many marriages are shaky, and it doesn't take much to topple them over."

> —MARVIN MITCHELSON, on celebrity divorces

"Only as a last resort."

—MAE WEST, on marriage

"It's okay."

—JON BON JOVI, on married life

"That's a matter of opinion."

—HERMIONE GINGOLD, twice divorced, when asked if her husband was alive

"Leave them while you're looking good."

—ANITA LOOS

"An archeologist is the best husband a woman can have; the older she gets, the more interested he is in her."

—AGATHA CHRISTIE, who was married to one

"In our family we don't divorce our men—we bury them."

—RUTH GORDON

"Oh, life is a glorious cycle of song, / A medley of extemporanea; / And love is a thing that can never go wrong; / And I am Marie of Romania."

—DOROTHY PARKER; Parker divorced, then remarried Alan Campbell

"I guess the only way to stop divorce is to stop marriage."

—WILL ROGERS

"It's amazing that all marriages don't end in divorce. If you can stay in love for more than two years, you're *on* something."

—FRAN LEBOWITZ

"When a marriage ends, who is left to understand it?"

—JOYCE CAROL OATES

201 Divorcé(e)s from A to Z

Kareem Abdul-Jabbar
Muhammad Ali
Woody Allen
Robert Altman
Julie Andrews
Alan Arkin
Desi Arnaz
Isaac Asimov
Lucille Ball
Anne Bancroft
Brigitte Bardot
George Benson
Carl Bernstein
Shirley Temple Black
Ivan Boesky
Napoleon Bonaparte
Bjorn Borg
David Bowie
Fannie Brice
David Brinkley
Mel Brooks
Anita Bryant
Richard Burton
Michael Caine

Ray Charles
Chevy Chase
Dick Clark
Natalie Cole
Sean Connery
Tom Cruise
Roger Daltrey
Bette Davis
Geena Davis
Doris Day
Catherine Deneuve
Robert De Niro
John Denver
Neil Diamond
Phil Donahue
Kirk Douglas
Bob Dylan
Clint Eastwood
Nora Ephron
Mia Farrow
Sally Field
Albert Finney
Carrie Fisher
Eddie Fisher

Ella Fitzgerald
F. Scott Fitzgerald
Malcolm Forbes
Betty Ford
Harrison Ford
Henry Ford II
Betty Furness
William Friedkin
Jerry Garcia
Judy Garland
James Garner
Jeff Goldblum
Samuel Goldwyn
Elliott Gould
Cary Grant
Merv Griffin
Alex Haley
Tom Hanks
Goldie Hawn
Hugh Hefner
Harry Helmsley
Leona Helmsley
Ernest Hemingway
Audrey Hepburn
Katharine Hepburn
Dustin Hoffman
Lena Horne
John Hurt
William Hurt
Barbara Hutton
Billy Idol
Julio Iglesias
Amy Irving
Mick Jagger
Billy Joel
Don Johnson
Michael Keaton
Edward Kennedy

Carole King
Larry King
Henry Kissinger
Calvin Klein
Jack Klugman
Stanley Kubrick
Burt Lancaster
Ann Landers
Michael Landon
Cloris Leachman
Frances Lear
Norman Lear
Janet Leigh
Jack Lemmon
John Lennon
David Letterman
Jerry Lewis
Ali MacGraw
Madonna
Lee Majors
Charles Manson
Penny Marshall
Dean Martin
Walter Matthau
Margaret Mead
Liza Minelli
Margaret Mitchell
Marilyn Monroe
Demi Moore
Dudley Moore
Mary Tyler Moore
Roger Moore
Paul Newman
Mike Nichols
Jack Nicholson
Nick Nolte
Laurence Olivier
Aristotle Onassis

Ryan O'Neal
Yoko Ono
Peter O'Toole
Dorothy Parker
Gregory Peck
Michelle Pfeiffer
Sidney Poitier
Elvis Presley
Richard Pryor
Roxanne Pulitzer
Anthony Quinn
Princess Lee Radziwill
Lou Rawls
Ronald Reagan
Vanessa Redgrave
Rob Reiner
Jason Robards, Jr.
Harold Robbins
Nelson Rockefeller
Ginger Rogers
Kenny Rogers
Mimi Rogers
Pete Rose
Diana Ross
Susan Sarandon
Vidal Sassoon
Telly Savalas
Charles Schulz
George C. Scott
George Segal
Tom Selleck
Omar Sharif
Cybill Shepherd
Dinah Shore
Carly Simon
Neil Simon
Paul Simon
O. J. Simpson

Wallis Warfield Simpson
Frank Sinatra
Upton Sinclair
Grace Slick
Tom Snyder
Bruce Springsteen
Sylvester Stallone
Ringo Starr
Rod Steiger
Sting
Barbra Streisand
Donna Summer
David Susskind
Donald Sutherland
James Taylor
Justice Clarence Thomas
Ted Turner
Tina Turner
Mike Tyson
Peter Ustinov
Jon Voight
Diane Von Furstenberg
Mike Wallace
Barbara Walters
Raquel Welch
Gene Wilder
Andy Williams
Hank Williams, Jr.
Paul Williams
Robin Williams
Flip Wilson
Dave Winfield
Shelley Winters
Jane Wyman
X (all divorcées are exes)
Loretta Young
Neil Young
Frank Zappa